THE PRINCIPLE

STRENGTH BASED SOBRIETY

DR. DAVID SUTTON

For information regarding permission, contact us at our website:
www.answeringaddiction.com,

or write to:

Answering Addiction
PO Box 3917
Sarasota, Florida 34230

TABLE OF CONTENTS

FOREWORD

BY ALAN TOBIASON

IT WAS IN JUNE OF 2006 that once again I found myself in a hospital trying to get sober. But this time it was different. I had almost lost my life. Three weeks of heavy binge drinking had put me in a coma. I couldn't believe it had happened again. Where was I? Not just physically, but how in the world had I gotten back here, in this terrible state! Not again?

I remember the fear that I felt…the confusion, the despair. My life and my battle with alcoholism and drug addiction, could be described like the experience of riding a roller coaster. My addiction took hold of me at the young age of 15, and I was hooked from the beginning. I was a "blackout drinker," that part I knew for sure.

Initially, the consequences were not too severe. But the longer I was in active addiction, the worse it became. The more the trouble, the greater the consequences. It had taken its toll and in 1989, I finally got sober. I would begin what was a ten-year period of sobriety. During this time, I rose through the ranks of our organization. Ultimately, I became the President of a large printing company near Chicago, Illinois. I had reached the "top of the mountain" only to realize it was the wrong one.

My story, though unique in its own circumstances, was not much different for those you hear in the rooms of recovery on any given day, in any city or town. I thought I had arrived; however, as it would be, I would drink again.

For the next six years my next encounter with active addiction was more intense than any before. There is a saying in recovery, "You have had in your life bad drinking days, but the worst drinking days are the ones ahead of you." That was, for sure, the case with me. Before it would come to an end, it had destroyed everything that was important to me. At this point, I felt I was never going to recover again. The best days of my life I felt were behind me. I had lost all hope for my future. In this book, David talks about the benefit of finding "hopelessness". My drinking had brought me to a state of being hopeless.

As most people discover that have gone back out to try drinking again, the second time getting sober was so much harder than the first time. I started going to meetings and was sober, but not really happy or feeling good about anything. For about a year, I stayed sober and went to meetings regularly, but my life was still in ruins. I had lost everything again and I had uncertainty about staying sober and life in general. I was floundering and my will to continue, to say the least, was not very strong.

Of all that I had lost, how I felt about myself was at the pinnacle. I am not sure I could even say I had one thing that was actually important to me. Something was missing. I felt empty inside and was living daily with a constant void. I had attended the best addiction treatment programs that money could buy but was still feeling lost. I was praying that God would reveal something…anything! I desperately needed something to change.

A friend had invited me to attend the Tuesday night addiction recovery lecture series at the Salvation Army, Center for Hope in Sarasota, Florida. I'm not sure why I agreed, but begrudgingly, I went. I had heard it all before at the meetings and was not really up to listening to the same old thing again.

I remember that first Tuesday night like it was yesterday. As we entered the parking lot, it was jam packed. The people getting out of their cars were buzzing. As we went in to look for seats, we found a full auditorium. I was amazed at the energy and enthusiasm of everyone. These people were excited for what they were about to experience.

When David entered the room, it was filled with shouts, applause, and a standing ovation. I remember feeling like I was at exactly the right place at exactly the right time. As David began to teach about the principles of recovery, I was amazed at his profound insight of the steps. I had never heard anyone, until this moment, speak with such authority. David would always end each session with the words "Welcome to Your New Life". I wanted this new life!

Never missing a Tuesday night, I would always invite others to join me. As I got to know David over the next few months, I knew I wanted what he had. What it was, I wasn't exactly sure, but he was happy about his sobriety! Every week I saw hundreds of clients at that program, making the connection and finding recovery.

At that time, David was the Director of the Center for Hope. Located in downtown Sarasota, it was home to over 200 people in their recovery programs. What I was to experience over the next years of my life, were the miracles of watching people who were the severest of alcoholics and drug addicts, "grab on" to the principles of recovery. I would see them change week to week. The transformation amazed me then, and still does today.

The programs that David developed, were in my opinion, the finest in the country. I can say that because I have been through some of the finest in the country. I began to volunteer working with the clients at the program. I started running classes and groups and working as a case manager.

As the programs grew, they branched out across the community and into the county jail. The Sarasota County Jail Recovery Pods became a tremendous venue for the programs to grow and provide a platform to teach others recovery. Not just don't drink and go to meetings, but the true pathway to permanent sobriety and a relationship with God.

In my prior 35 years working in the marketplace, I have had many teachers, leaders, and bosses. No single person has influenced my life more than David. Our friendship has grown over the years. It is one built with mutual respect and encouragement. My experience is that God will put the right person into your life at the right time. God has provided everything I have needed and more, for my life, sobriety and friendships.

Today I own and operate Purpose House Transitional homes. We have 120 residents in our long-term recovery sober homes. They are put together and operate on the principles I learned in those Tuesday night classes, many years ago. We practice these principles of recovery in all our affairs.

The meetings are still important. I am still teaching classes on addiction recovery. We now oversee a Celebrate Recovery program with hundreds of people in attendance every Sunday night. Of course, among the teachers is my friend, Dr. David. I still learn so much from the classes, his books, and from his example.

Today I have the New Life that David welcomed us to each week. It is a life that I never could have dreamt possible. Now as David approaches his 40th year of sobriety, he has given us another gift entitled,

"The Principle Approach, 40 Years Later."

I trust this book will be as meaningful, practical and life-changing as it has been to me. By the way... **Welcome to your New Life.**

INTRODUCTION

RECENTLY I HEARD A WOMAN say, "I'm one day closer to the next drink than I was yesterday." "Only an arms length away from the next drink?" Not the first time I have heard that statement. Really, after many years of sobriety, how can that be?

My entry into the life of recovery was a tumultuous one. I started the first time when I was only 19 years old. I look back and see I should have been addressing my addiction many years before that. I moved in and out of not drinking and using drugs until I was 27. Finally I was ready to surrender.

An old fellow told me that I was approaching it backwards. He said, "You come into the meetings and you set the bottle down somewhere in the future, and every day you are here you are taking a set closer to the next time you pick up. What I would suggest is you set the bottle down, turn around and begin to walk away from it. Put distance between you and the next drink". Some really sound advise.

So in 1980 I did that. I have been steadily moving in the opposite direction of the drink and the drugs every since. I'm not closer to a drink today than I was yesterday. I have steadily moved 40 years toward sobriety. For me to just randomly pick up a drink is not the issue. If I were to go back it would be a calculated change of direction, and a purposefully undoing of what I learned, believed and experienced.

I guess it is a matter of which way your walking. I chose to separate myself, detached from a drink or any substitute, and I have not turned around to move in the other direction yet.

We can keep falling off the cliff, only if we stay close to the edge. You can fall off the cliff and lay at the bottom waiting for an ambulance to come and rescue you, or build a fence on the top of the cliff so you stop falling off. It is really up to you how you approach it. I know where the edge of the cliff is and have chosen not only build a fence on the top, but to move far away from it.

For me to get to the next drink I would need to turn around and walk over the tapestry made up of my 40 years of meetings I've attended, years of working a step process, sponsors who I have known and learned from, decades of classes I've taught, books I've read, prayers I've prayed and answers He's made.

That is a lot to overcome to get back to a drink. If I have learned one thing it is this. I know where I set down the last drink, it has never moved. I know where the next drink is, should I ever lose my mind and decide to drink, it is right along side the last one.

I know where I set down the last drink, it has never moved.

I have written this book partly out of gratitude for my years of sober life and partly out of a desire to give to those looking for answers to staying sober. However it mostly out of a heart desire to fulfill Gods plan for my life. This is part of it.

The first "Principle Approach" book, "The Keys to Recovery" was about the steps and the corresponding principles. I would recommend it and The "Principle Approach Workbook" as a tool for working the steps. This is a new "Principle Approach" book called "Strength Based Sobriety".

There are ideas in here that I have gained from years of going to meetings and listening to others talk about their recovery from addiction. The books I have read are so valuable to growth. God will always reveal more, if we are open minded, willing to listen and allow new ideas to fill our minds.

Those who read this are going to find things that they agree with and others things that they don't. The topics I've written about are out of my experience. Each chapter is written as a stand alone subject, but is included as part of the collective whole. The reader will be challenged to think through the ideas and make his or her own conclusions.

Two rednecks, Leroy and Bubba are out in the woods hunting. They had been drinking all day and were pretty drunk.

All at once, Bubba starts stumbling around and finally collapses. Leroy hollers over to him and says, "Bubba, is you all right?" He gets no answer.

He staggers over to him and checks and Bubba is not breathing. Leroy checks his eyes and they are already glazed over.

So Leroy whips out his cell phone and calls 911.

The lady answers, "911, what is your emergency?"

"Hey, this is Leroy and I think my buddy is dead!" he yells.

"What can I do?"

The operator says, "Calm down. First, let's make sure he's dead."

Leroy slurs ok, wait just a minute.

There's silence, then a gunshot.

Back on the phone, Leroy says, "OK, now what's next?"

CHAPTER 1

STRENGTH BASED RECOVERY

IN THE SHORT 40 YEARS of my applied study about those struggling with addiction, my conclusion is that the face of addiction has changed. The culture and the context of how we address addiction needs to be considered in our presentation of recovery. The days of don't drink and go to meetings as a stand-alone solution have faded. In the repository of the great thinking of our day, we see that the severity of addiction has increased. If we are to keep pace with the ever-growing need, then we must rise to the occasion and find wisdom for the day.

Information, just because it is clever or rhymes, does not insure correctness. Repeating an inaccuracy does not cause it to be true. Examination of the subject uncovers those who are rigid and resistant to any addiction other than alcohol. They make clear the distinction between addictions but accept all dimensions of unproven thought as the solution. Adamant about the singleness of purpose, their rigidity turns away the very people who will be the torchbearers of the sobriety of tomorrow.

Proficiency in life-giving and life-changing recovery is the distinction between those who will carry forward the great message of sobriety and those who will fade into a memory of what used to be. What was it like back in the day, really? You speak of the time before the pill epidemic? Before the crack culture, before brains were toasted by bath salts and spice? Before someone was dying of a heroin overdose every weekend?

The pioneers of recovery anticipated a day when finding a plain old garden variety drunk would be difficult. That day is now. Will we rise to the occasion and have help available for everyone or fade with visions of yesterday with a one size fits all answer?

And what of those who resist the idea of God and faith-based solutions? They will be self-eliminated as those who fail to see the changing need. Sobriety without connecting to faith and finding God's intervention has failure written across the doorpost. No reason to even go there. God can and will bring freedom from addiction if we seek him.

You cannot move to the next chapter by reading the past chapter over and over. Where we have been is only a measure of the things we have tried. It should not become the final prognosticator of where we are headed. To my knowledge, there is still no miracle cure for addictions. Numerous plans, processes and claims have helped some, but the addiction epidemic is still that - a growing epidemic. The overdose rates are higher than I have seen in my lifetime. Which, by the way, is now measured in decades rather than years.

While there are many forms of treatment for addiction, in this era we have seen an escalation in addictions of all forms. The general ideas for addressing addiction issues are often a singular focus, disregarding the multifaceted nature of the matter.

For example, the mental health constituency, with all their wonderful efforts, really only focus on the issues of diagnosable mental health challenges. They offer medication designed to limit symptomatic behavioral issues and most often some therapeutic forms of counseling, possibly followed by the recommendation to go to A.A. Rather than dealing with all of the core issues, they only approach a singular aspect of addictive behavior.

You cannot move to the next chapter, by reading the past chapter over and over.

If addiction is only a chemical imbalance in the brain, this type of application might prove to be effective. However, addiction is equally a mental obsession. The mental obsession cannot be effectively addressed with an occasional or even weekly counseling session. Understanding that it is a daily obsession should help make it clear that focusing on correction with a weekly treatment plan is likely to fall short.

Addiction is also an emotional malady. Emotions are seldom connected to time frames. Feelings last longer than a day, a week or even a year. Some are for a lifetime. If a person is battling the emotional imbalance of addiction, it cannot be addressed by occasional intervention, but needs uninterrupted support. To have any lasting impact, having access to help becomes a daily necessity.

One of the clear indicators of an effective treatment program is understanding the time application. Often, we try to treat an addiction on a weekly basis, though it's a daily problem, and often a moment to moment problem.

Addiction is also spiritual in its nature. A spiritual condition or state of being, is not constricted by time. The nature of spiritual matters is actually timeless. The only effective way to address a spiritual challenge is through disciplines that impact a person's daily routine.

So, let me start with Common Sense Sobriety, practical and uncomplicated. Life for healthy people is often complicated. For addictive people an additional complication is that they are always a little out of touch with reality, both in their thinking and behavior, complicated without the outside influences. Their choices are often very questionable, quite self-centered and at times downright ridiculous, adding to the confusion.

A spiritual condition or state of being, is not constricted by time.

There forms around recovery circles and programs, a natural gravitation to making recovery from addiction equally confusing and complicated. I have observed that the simplest solutions are really the answers that most people, trying to find recovery, find most beneficial.

This is the place where great thinkers may need to do an about face. The answers are not at the top of the psychological malaise, nor in the deep recesses of the world of meditation or medication. They are not even found in the far-reaching theological formulas, which provide much truth, but often not the much-needed relief.

Recovery is found in the simple wisdom of how someone else has found a repose from their addiction. We eliminate the mental gymnastics and embrace the simple conclusions that keep us sober and moving forward to the joy of real life. The seemingly insignificant one liner or slogan often makes all the difference.

So, let's explore the simple paths that would receive a "yes vote" from the average reasonable person looking in from the outside. Many of the very things that could bring temporary relief and permanent change were tried and for one reason or another failed. Often, it's not the failure of the solution or the recovery concept itself; but the personal effort is where we come up short. A person making an honest, wholehearted effort in applying the solution succeeds, where another takes a half-hearted questionable attempt to apply the concept and fails.

We often, without really trying, throw out an idea as failed, because someone tried it and met with dismal results. We toss our not only the baby with the bath water, we also throw out the soap, wash cloth and the tub. All to be replaced with a more complex way of getting clean. (Did you catch the play on words?)

With all that we have learned, why is there an increase in those who are addicted?

I have heard, "I tried a 12 Step Program and I just didn't fit in. Or I went to a 28-day rehab and got high on the way home. I tried church and it just did not work. They told me I was no longer an alcoholic, so I thought I could drink safely." It is likely not what you tried, but how you tried it that created the failure.

I am not saying that the experts don't know the intricacies of addictions well enough. There are volumes of wonderful information about every manner of addiction, that afflicts every segment of our population. There is the physiological approach providing therapy for the emotional and mental needs, the medical approach providing short term symptomatic relief, though often creating additional addictions.

We have addressed the legal ramifications and added serious consequences to motivate people into recovery. We have analyzed family and community impact and even the spiritual dynamics, as we have studied addictions.

I for one, am happy that we have progressed so far in our understanding. That being said, check the statistics. With all that we have learned, why is there an increase in those who are addicted and a very minuscule success rate in most addiction programs?

So here we are, and after a long time of studying addictions, I have given up studying addictions. I've decided to study recovery. The addiction studies demonstrating weakness and deficiencies have been done and overdone. Perhaps we should move our focus to the strengths that can and will emerge when we walk away from addiction. Only then can we begin to build our lives into what they were designed to be from the beginning before we became addicted.

I cannot continue believing that the majority of those addicted were born that way. Are there indicators that some of this might be hereditary or genetic? In some cases, yes. But a large number that I have met, in all manner of addiction programs, have no such family history link. They appear to be the only alcoholic, the singular drug addict, the lone member of the family addicted to food. You do remember hearing about "the black sheep of the family"?

Even if you inherited a gene that gave you a propensity toward addiction, that does not necessarily need to define your future. We are all created with strengths and weaknesses. Overcoming weaknesses requires discipline, direction, and faith; regardless of who we are or where we come from. We all build strengths through study, application, and practice. We develop our skills and make our life into what it was intended to be. The idea that I was just born this way, so I can do nothing about it is erroneous. This is a victim mentality and it becomes a restraint to finding true freedom.

You cannot get well and be the victim at the same time.

So, let's simplify this. Set aside the "how" you became addicted and the "why" you got hooked and simply accept the fact that you did. Remember, often a simple solution is better. It eliminates the paralysis of analysis.

Let's face it, pain never produces change, it only produces the desire to change. Knowledge and information can produce change but not without doing something with it. Time doesn't bring about change. There are old alcoholics and there are young people in sobriety. If time heals all wounds, like some believe, then God is not required, and neither are recovery programs. Need does not produce change. There are 20-year-old ".com billionaires" and 75-year-old hard working people without a dime. Need doesn't really produce change, only the desire to change.

If all the losses in life are a logical and valid reasoning for leaving addiction, why don't people just quit? Remember, many years ago, there was a slogan, "Just say no". It was a great thought but it didn't work. Certainly, the reasons to quit are good, as far as they go. So is digging into life failures and identifying what went wrong; it is an imperative.

However, the truth is that this approach to recovery comes up short. It is based on a mental, emotional, and spiritual picture that is best described as a "vulnerability model". It is the way up from the bottom of the pit we have dug for our life and a good place to start. But is that all there is? This approach focuses on identifying our individual weaknesses and controlling them. If we do this, ultimately, it should prevent our return to active addiction.

This is really what has become the standard for relapse prevention. This has been the buzz phrase regarding addictions in the mental health field for a long time. The vulnerability model is the predominant method embraced by those who access a limited recovery, just to return to their addiction. Falling back into active using after a period of recovery is common and happens to people of all ages, walks of life and lengths of sobriety.

Time doesn't bring about change; it does reveal the ongoing need to change and the truth that we are stuck where we are.

I have taught methods and ideas to prevent falling back into addiction for many years. Mainly focusing on the personal failure, while not identifying the deeper problems of the heart. Basically, this teaching provides a focus on the method of entry into recovery, by focusing on why it is wrong and learning to control it. This is a primary approach to entry level sobriety, and for what it is, it is good.

In general, the relapse prevention idea focuses on the things that will take us out of sobriety. Perceptions and memories that are connected to people, places, and things. Cravings, both physical and mental. All of those obsessive, recurring thought processes of drinking or using, we call "stinkin thinkin".

We could also add remorse over our financial and relationship losses. Let's be clear. You will not stay sober for the things you have lost. Much of what we have known and things we have possessed, we will never get back. Many of the opportunities that were squandered in a life of addiction are actually gone forever.

So, we work the steps and embrace the processes of recovery. After a time, we see nowhere else to take our personal growth, so we redirect and re-energize our efforts and look more closely at our weaknesses. All of this is done in an attempt to find further layers of disfunction and failure.

Some refer to the process with the old adage of peeling an onion. It is just one layer at a time. A long, laborious, and never-ending process. But let me ask you, "What if you get to the core and discover you are an onion?" "Do you just continue to emanate odor and be offensive?" Come on, man! There are enough challenges to getting clean and sober without looking for deeper problems.

Many are stuck in the problem - -
while ignoring the solution.

Searching deep for anything that resembles progress or change so we feel good about ourselves. However, in the process of our introspection, we will run into momentary behavioral failures.

Often these are seen as an indicator that they must still be really sick and consider this as being perpetually dysfunctional. This is being stuck in the problem (vulnerability centered addiction) while ignoring the solution (strength-based recovery).

This is like a person who buys a plane ticket just to hear the free safety lecture. Showing up but not really going anywhere. Those battling out of the cycle of addiction should not settle for just finding methods of abstinence. Not using but still daily battling with all the dysfunctional behaviors.

I would submit that there is a better approach to prevent the recurring addiction. Rather than "failure avoidance", which desperately focuses on not falling back, why not turn it around and begin to focus on what is necessary for growing into permanent sobriety and success? Not just a survival sobriety with the avoidance of picking up but building a life that does not include the option of returning to addiction. I see this as a paradigm shift from relapse prevention to sobriety preservation or "Strength Based Recovery". This is not simply an exercise in semantics, but a total realignment of focus and a restructure of our priorities.

"Strength Based Recovery" is setting aside the deep, sometimes redundant introspection, used in identifying weakness and instead, beginning the journey into finding and embracing our strengths. Not that searching our hearts and minds for the reality of our failed life is not an important priority. However, long-term introspection cannot make us stronger. It simply solidifies our future struggles based on our past experience.

The past failures, at some juncture, become the prognosticator of our future; one marked with weakness, an unchanged character and weak, anemic faith. Rather than continuing this self-perpetuating focus on failure, wouldn't it make more sense to identify our abilities, prioritize our goals and reinforce our strengths?

Some people have ten years of sobriety; others have one year of sobriety that they have repeated ten times.

I formally went through the 12 Step process in 1981 and I completed each in its respective order. From working the step process, I have gained recovery principles that I have lived by, and now for a lifetime, I have invested in. My end-result was not to become more and more introspective. No, no, a hundred times no!

A focus on my weaknesses only serves to make them become more prominent. You cannot rid yourself of fear or anger, lust, or greed by focusing on these defective parts of your personality. Identify them? Yes. Deal with the behaviors? Yes, again. But to make a lifetime focus on the weaknesses only serves to further establish the challenge. We begin to self-identify, who we are, by the very weaknesses we are trying to overcome.

A better approach is to work through the steps in order to access the principles. These principles then become the foundation for a life of freedom. Redirecting our focus to these life principles will give us the impetus to build something positive.

Once the steps have been honestly worked with the goal of establishing these principles in your life, you can then simply live them. We can then practice these principles in all aspects of our lives. The steps still remain. For they are the key for redefining and regaining access to any principle that we have lost sight of. Further, they also become a ready tool for helping others.

But working the steps over and over will only serve to keep us trapped in perpetual victimization. Many have become victims of their character defects. They blame character defects and give themselves permission to remain broken, weak, and trapped in the ideals of early recovery. Some people have ten years of sobriety; others have one year of sobriety that they have repeated ten times.

We should see the steps more like the scaffolding that is necessary to build a structure. The scaffolding used to build the new building was never designed to become synonymous with the structure. Having completed the building, the scaffolding comes down. It may be used again and again for cleaning, repairing, and painting the structure, but it never becomes part of the structure. Focusing on our weaknesses and defects is somewhat like choosing to move in and set up house on the scaffolding when there is an entire building in which to reside.

Many have become a victim of their character defects.

I believe that a focus on fear and failure has an essential role to play in identifying and breaking down the denial that is so prevalent in addictions. However, I submit for your consideration, that after a lifetime of focusing on fear and failure, we discover it only produces after its kind — more fear and more failure.

A redirection towards faith and progress is the only true way to grow past the entry level of recovery. This beginning place of a sober, spiritual life is not the endgame, but only the entry point. The change of direction repositions us from the law of "diminishing return" into the law of "exponential increase".

We start with our vulnerability and our weakness with a goal of moving into a robust "Strength Based Recovery".

Strength Based Recovery moves us from one level to another.

	From:	**To:**
1.	Nurturing weaknesses.	Building strengths.
2.	Defeatist mentality.	More than a conqueror's mindset.
3.	Scarcity mindset.	God's limitless resources.

4.	Identifying problems.	Grasping solutions.
5.	Spiritual uncertainty.	Spiritual confidence.
6.	Hearing life's challenges.	Hearing God's plan.
7.	Self-pity.	Value of our life.
8.	Directional quagmire.	Purpose and goals.
9.	Life limitations.	Options to change.
10.	Mental bondage.	Foundational freedoms.

We offer hope to the hopeless. However, hope that is given without opportunity is simply being mean. Hope to change, hope to grow, hope to recover, and genuinely get your life on track is needed. However, without offering this manner of a workable, practical life application, hope becomes a hollow promise.

The option to move into strength based recovery:

1. Is normally greater than our response is to it.
2. Grows in proportion to what you are doing with it.
3. Is outside normal human understanding.
4. The call to grow in recovery, stops if there is no response.
5. Is accessed through diligent effort toward personal development.
6. Requires deep interpersonal healing.
7. Is available to everyone who will, by faith, give it an honest effort.

Let's put away our illusions of success and embrace true freedom.

- You can get well and be whole.
- You can find permanent sobriety.
- You can become comfortably sober.

It is a simple process. At times not easy, but simple. Overcoming the complexities of getting sober, as many have, is a matter of choosing to change our focus.

Knowledge produces change.
Divine knowledge produces permanent change.

This pastor received a parrot as a gift. Problem was that the parrot had a bad attitude and an even worse vocabulary. Every word out of the bird's mouth was rude, obnoxious, and laced with profanity.

The pastor tried and tried to change the bird's attitude by teaching the bird scripture verses, playing worship music and anything else he could think of to straighten out the bird's vocabulary, but with no success.

Finally, the pastor was had enough and he yelled at the parrot. The parrot yelled back. The pastor shook the parrot and the parrot got angrier and even more vulgar. In desperation, John threw up his hands, grabbed the bird and put him in the freezer. For a little while the parrot squawked, pecked at the door, and yelled. Then suddenly, there was total silence. Not a sound was heard for several minutes.

Compassion kicked in and suddenly the pastor thought that he might have killed the parrot. So he opened the door to the freezer. The parrot calmly stepped out onto the pastors outstretched arm.

The parrot cleared his throat and said, "I believe I may have offended you with my bad language and bad attitude. I am sincerely remorseful for my inappropriate transgressions and I fully intend to do everything I can to adjust my unconscionable and unforgivable behavior."

The pastor was stunned at the change in the bird's attitude. So he asked the parrot what had made such a dramatic change in his behavior.

Without hesitation the parrot replied, "May I ask what the chicken did?"

CHAPTER 2

POINTS OF RESISTANCE:

THE FALLACY OF HAVING A cure for addictions is not a new idea. Occasionally I come across someone who has an idea that they are the one that will be able to produce the cure. There is a pill on the market that is touted as the cure for alcoholics; take this pill and all of your cravings for alcohol disappear. If it were only a physical challenge, then the pill would probably be effective. By observation and as a person with an addictive nature, addicts will often switch addictions. So, if you cure an addiction on the surface, the core issues will become the seedbed for some other addiction.

Because of the nature of the mental obsession of addiction, the core issue of seeking something that makes me feel better must be dealt with. There is, of course, the vast implications of a spiritual deficiency attached to addiction that a pill would not address.

In the world of recovery, we call addiction a "disease of more". One is good, two is better, three has to be great. I have experienced this in my life regardless of what behavior is being addressed. It was that way with alcohol, it was that way when I smoked cigarettes, it was the case with food and even physical activities.

The "never enough" mindset can never be cured with a pill.

Others claim processes like acupuncture, hypnosis and even yoga are the answer to addiction. These may work for aspects of addiction. But if they were the true cure, I would think there would be evidence of great numbers of people jumping on board. So far, I have not met any.

In the church realm, many people believe that the cure for addiction is spiritual. If you get Jesus in your life, this addiction will disappear. Unfortunately, as a believer and a minister, I have watched the opposite happen over and over.

I am not denying anyone's testimony or God's power. But truthfully, I have seen men and women of great spiritual stature and strength, caught up in addiction even after many years of ministering to others.

Let me relate the story of dear friend of mine, who for many years served as a prominent international minister. Loving, kind, dutiful and a tremendous speaker and writer. She never had any demonstrable addiction issues. Her health required that she have a series of surgeries. After prolonged illness, she ended up addicted to pain pills. It ultimately ended her effectiveness, ministry, and life. Even those who showed no prior signs of addictive behavior have ended up caught in the trap of addiction.

I know several pastors who have come out of alcoholism and drug addiction and have served in the church faithfully. These are people with hearts to serve God and help others. But when life happened and stress came later they were lured into thinking they could drink with impunity. Only to find out that once they picked up the first drink, they were off and running again.

A member of our Board of Directors, whom I have known for over

30 years, tells this story. He was a worship leader and a pastor, successful businessman, and an exceptional family man, a loyal husband and dedicated father.

He had accumulated 25 years of sobriety. He was on vacation with his family, enjoying the benefits of a life well lived. Without much thought, he decided to have a margarita. He was in very short order off and running again. It was many years before he came to the end of this spree.

He now has been clean and sober once again for 10 years. He is still a very godly man, with a great family. The difference is that he has acquired a much deeper understanding of alcoholism. He now has firsthand experience that there is no cure for addiction. There is a reprieve and relief that can last a lifetime, but in my observation, no one who has been a chronic alcoholic is later on able to become a social or occasional drinker. We are never cured; our addiction is only put into remission.

What are the telltale signs that mark a relapse? What are the sticking points that would cause a person to go backwards? Why, after finding a solution to a life destroying, uncontrollable behavior, would a person choose to go back? I would submit that it is more than surrendering to the drink or the drugs but a surrender reaching past the walls of resistance. This takes us to what I call the points of resistance. Searching our lives to find these unchanged behaviors and beliefs will require an ongoing, perhaps daily self-inventory.

Relevance and Disruption

The more I know, the more I can recognize the vast array of what is left to learn. What I know is not a bad thing, unless I choose to ignore it, fail to apply it, or allow my selfishness to override what I have learned.

An inventory that is of much value must contain relevance. While discovering the history of bad behavior, it must bring us to current behaviors and applying it to our daily living. Relevance means that what we have discovered, has application to us right where we live.

Even more necessary for success, our inventory must create disturbance. We disrupt the hidden places of secret thinking and behavior, in order to break free from their strangle hold.

How does that work? I cannot change what I cannot see. Even when I'm fully aware of the need to change, an about-face correction may be challenging. The things hidden from me are often apparent to others. Many of the hidden things were hidden on purpose from others by me. This is self-protection. However, after a time, the thoughts and behaviors hidden from others become lost in the self-deception. Eventually what I hide from other people will become concealed in such a clandestine way that it is invisible to me.

We are quick to embrace the idea that our fourth step, life inventory, is designed to create in us the ability to see what has kept us from relationships with other people. Family, work and business or those that we interchange with on a casual basis, shopping, doctors or even at church.

As we take a daily inventory of ourselves, we must identify the barriers and the points of resistance that were reinforced by our failures and faulty beliefs. This applies to staying sober, as well as to building a healthy interchange with the world around us. This internal review must contain this life relevance.

What may be more necessary for success in our daily inventory is disruption. We must disrupt the hidden pockets of resistance, in order to break free from their strangle hold.

Points of resistance exist in everyone but are unique to each person. Exclusive to our individualized personality, life perspective and set of beliefs. They are influenced by our experiences in life, failures and abuses, successes, and joys.

We will uncover our points of resistance if we take the time to review honestly. These are truths about our life that we subconsciously, yet actively resist admitting. No one favors being forced to look at something that challenges who we see ourselves to be. This includes our perception of the world, our beliefs about life, and quite often, our very sense of identity.

These areas of resistance mask patterns of behavior that cause repeated failure. They block interchange with others and prohibit building healthy partnerships with others on any level. The greater challenge is that they create internal barriers that foster our negative self-talk and create in us a defeatist imagery.

Layered Denial

We resist even the awareness of our own maneuvers used to avoid what is challenging our perception. This I refer to as "multi-leveled denial". We resist not only the core issue, but the stimulus that compels our awareness of these challenges. Characterized as "defense mechanisms", we use these forms of denial to keep at bay what we do not want to face.

We are reticent to examine our deeply held, underlying beliefs about ourselves. However, if not addressed in the inventory process, the things we are trying to hide will be seen. Our emotions will often betray us. Not being able to mask the feelings, anger, fear, pride, and isolation will disclose what we wanted to suppress and hide, and what we fear to verbalize. Take a closer look at denial.

Denial:

1. Denial is refusing to know what you already know.
2. Denial is part of the fabric of our design as human

beings, for it allows us to function until we are able to receive and face the truth.

3. Denial is a form of self-preservation that protects us from looking directly at the truth all at once. It allows us to function on a lower level or with a diminished capacity until we can accept greater truths about ourselves.
4. Denial itself is not the problem, but rather its overuse or underuse.
5. Denial is the first point of resistance.
6. Denial is bliss. Pretending what I already know doesn't exist.
7. Denial is a form of the 5th Amendment clause. I exercise my right to refuse to speak of what I already know. Knowing that to speak of it will become a form of self-incrimination. Of course, while there is no visible incrimination from silence, sometimes the silence itself tells a story.

The opposite is also true. Acceptance is choosing to acknowledge what I already know. The personal inventory is much like counsel and even therapy. It is clarifying motives, facing facts, and ultimately embracing what I already know.

We must identify the varied points of resistance that distort our perspective from reality, hamper our basic relationship functionality, obstruct association and connection with others.

As with people, but on a greater scale, we find these points of resistance have kept us from embracing a relationship with God and fostering a spiritual life. This level of interchange is where true life transformation comes from. This spiritual resistance is far more dangerous and damaging than that of resistance toward others.

The touch points (resistance points) that have kept us trapped in a faulty beliefs system and perception of the world need to be uncovered, explored, and ultimately eradicated.

Resistance Points:

The barriers that hindered your initial inventory, will plague your continuation towards sobriety. The things you skipped over and refused to look at will always resurface. What blocked your spiritual advancement will buffer any progressive, ongoing spiritual review, and limit your spiritual growth and strengthening. We do not remain spiritually infantile and weak without reasons.

11 Things That Will Block You From Sober Maturity:

1. **Layered Denial:** Denying not only the core issue, but ignoring the secretive maneuvers used to avoid facing the very challenges that highlight the fact that something is wrong.
2. **Internalized Defiance:** The unspoken protests that occur when we feel we are being told what to do, how to think or how to behave. It is this internal dissent that creates what I refer to as "self-talk insistence" contrary to what is being presented or suggested. The famous, I will not …., you can't tell me …., you can't make me ….. Refusing to participate even though we were planning on it originally. Expected in children, yes, but you are an adult. Come on man! You're not a kid anymore.
3. **Exoneration Refusal:** Clinging to unreasonable, obsolete grudges. Not forgiving when there appears a logical, sensible reason to do so. We hold on, not so much to the un-forgiveness, as much as to the underlying hurt. Often, concealed guilt is at the core. Not disclosing wrongs I have inadvertently

or knowingly committed, creates an impediment to setting right the breach between myself and another. They owe me.

4. **Authorized Character Defects:** This is giving myself permission to violate my own standards and participate in old behavior patterns. Permission is granted based on the false claim that I don't have the ability to control my behavior. There is a vast difference between purposefully engaging a behavior and just missing the mark. This is actively knowing I'm in violation of what I actually believe is right.

5. **Unjustifiable Anger:** This is being angry without a reason. The scripture talks about being angry without a cause. So, there is some anger that is to be anticipated and is acceptable when processed correctly. In these cases, how we act out our anger is more of the point, controlling your responses and even your reactions. Your words may not get you into immediate trouble but will start the ball rolling. Being angry in a general sort of way is different from being angry all the time with a sense of entitlement and self-excusal.

6. **Disappointment Pathos:** Pathos is emotion, passion, feeling, sentiment, deep sadness. Somehow, we have become disappointed and are suffering with disillusionment. This disappointment is often with people. We have an expectation of how others will react toward us, lend us help or generally treat us. Wrong expectations lay the groundwork for resentments and broken relationships.

   Disappointment pathos includes disenchantment with our beliefs. We create in our mind a belief and an understanding that fits us well. Not reality, but imagination. Again, expectations of God doing what we want him to do may not be reality. By the way, this is all your doing. Understand that in order to have disappointment first requires appointment. Who appointed you that you are now un-appointed or disappointed?

7. **Caustic Fear:** There is normal fear that everyone encounters. Some fear is healthy. Caustic fear is abrasive, is bitter, cutting and corroding. This caustic fear wears away resistance and destroys slowly without immediate impact or notice. Fear of people. Fear of poverty. Fear of failure. It is a paralyzingly angst or constant aversion. The measurable damage accumulates over time. It always increases and always damages that which is healthy and wholesome.

8. **Constituent Analyzation:** This is taking other people's inventory. In doing so, we are making the presumption that we know all the facts and motives. Assuming we know their thoughts and motives, we make judgements on them. It usually follows that we compare ourselves to them. We most often find our self-picture as better than them or lessor than them. Either way, it is not a true assessment and will create relationship distortions. Keep in mind that taking someone's inventory is always a taking process and never a giving one.

9. **Conflicting Desires:** Common to most people, this is especially significant in the addictive personality. Wanting two or more of anything that are contradictory to one another. A wife and a girlfriend, a new car and being debt free, more time with the family and sitting at the bar. Addicts seem to have difficulty making positive choices; they want what they want, when they want it, usually at any cost.

10. **Imminent Calamity:** It is apprehension, uneasiness, restlessness, and some forms of disquiet. Something bad is going to happen, a sense of impending doom. Negative assertions become obsessive thinking and hold an enslaving, oppressing, power, and control over our life advancement.
11. **Displaced Regret:** There is a German word Weltschmerz pronounced with a v sound, veltshmerts. It is a sorrow that one feels and accepts as one's necessary portion in life, sentimental pessimism. These are regrets we have that are simply hidden away. They form self-concepts that are not true. We attach fate, bad luck, or even Divine providence to the outcomes.

The essence of our recovery inventory is to first identify the people that we have wronged. Secondly, to clarify how circumstance and situations have impacted us and how we have in turn impacted others through our faulty behavior. But that should not be the ending of the exercise.

The goal of the initial inventory is the development of a process that allows us a lifelong skill of self-review. This increases the possibility of keeping our side of the street clean both with people and with God. is not the end of the matter.

The Spiritual Inventory

I have encountered many in the pathway of sobriety that desire a greater spiritual emphasis in their program of recovery. It alludes them for the lack of taking on the spiritual part of inventory. Is this not the beginning point for a lifetime of spiritual growth? Without a routine inventory, our spiritual life becomes stagnant, anemic and quite boring. Without an inventory, we will lose the momentum and synergism that makes a spiritual life exciting, dynamic, and powerful.

Complacency, apathy, and spiritual pride become the hallmark of a person who claims spiritual progress but refuses spiritual inventory. If we claim spiritual progress, then there needs be an active and accurate measure of our spiritual life and personal growth.

The personal inventory is not always a moral dialogue between the voices of right and wrong; sometimes it is a desperate deliberation between hope and fear. Hope of reward and fear of consequences. Herein lie the pockets of resistance.

We reconcile the internal conflict by rationalizing our behavior. We do so with the knowledge that God understands my weakness and will show mercy and not judgement. We attempt to hold two opposing views. "I know this is wrong, but I want it anyway. It will make me feel better." This is known as "cognitive dissonance". It is a lack of harmony in our reasoning, our comprehension, and even our perception.

We want to trust that God is good and will never leave us or forsake us, yet sometimes we dare not bank our lives on this for fear of disappointment. This is doubt. This is "Spiritual Dissonance".

In understanding resistance, the person finds it hard to believe and is most challenged at the very point where he or she most needs and perhaps wants to believe. This is not a coincidence. The mental and emotional hurt derived from both cognitive and spiritual dissonance comes from the clash between the desire to believe and the fear to believe. These opposing ideas create a distraction and tend to glaze over old wounds found at the core of resistance.

Diminishing Return and Exponential Increase

A final point of resistance is that I want the result of hard work without the labor. The primary reason people fail to maintain sobriety is broken focus. Broken focus produces double vision or trying to move in two directions at one time. Moving toward sobriety or moving back to our addiction. Left unaddressed and un-inventoried, ultimately the addiction will win.

It is necessary to have a vision of recovery, to embrace it and to develop it, because without a vision of recovery, the romance of the high or drink will take over.

There has been a pattern of "diminishing return" that we tend to forget about. This can be replaced by a new design called "exponential increase". But not without an honest routine inventory.

So, there is a law of "diminishing return" regarding the addiction to alcohol, drugs and of course, other addictions. Regardless of what your "drug of choice" is, gambling, pornography, even electronics (yes, people are addicted to the little hand-held devices regardless of the brand name), there is a matter of diminishing return.

When you first begin your innocent venture, it takes a much smaller amounts of your drug of choice, to get the desired effect. The longer you are involved, the more it will take to get the same effect, or even a lesser result. In fact, it often becomes the case that it requires a lot of whatever your drug of choice is just to stay normal.

Of course, this applies to anything that we do for self-gratification. We are looking for the thing that will fill the void and sometimes we find the thing that seems to do the trick.

For example, choose a hobby. Any hobby you have had will do. Go look in the garage or the attic and see the skeletal remains of many hobbies of days gone by. Try to exhume them and start up again. See if you can find the passion that was there when you went crazy doing the "whatever the latest craze was back in the day" project. This was "the project to end all projects!" It would perhaps someday become so much a part of your life that you would open a business and make it your life's work. While you are rooting around out there, forgive yourself for all the junk you bought in the multi-level business. You know the one your brother-in-law got you started in because you were both going to be rich? So, what happened? The law of diminishing return. You found out that the effort was not worth the payoff.

In addiction, you eventually found out the pleasure wasn't worth the pain that followed. Sometimes it was just too late to walk away. What you needed to get you there no longer worked. The new levels seemed to bring out new devils. The thrill is gone. The "drug of choice" that you depended on was too soon to become your enemy and even your tormentor. The return was steadily decreasing and the requirement was incrementally becoming larger.

Everything that you give from your life really does not exit your life, it simply enters your future.

On the flip side to that equation is another law which is the law of "exponential increase". This is activated anytime that you begin to involve yourself in the process of doing for others and denying your own desires. It is not necessary to measure the increase, it just happens. It is connected to your spiritual life and is clearly a part of God's plan for your activities.

Everything that you are involved in, that is by design for the benefit of others, begins to bring increase. Everything that you desire for your life is linked to giving to others. All that you give from your life really does not exit your life, it simply enters your future. The best part is that it never enters your future the way it was when you gave it. As you freely help someone else, it is multiplied and always at an increased rate. This "exponential increase" is actually the mirror opposite of the law of "diminishing return".

Are you tired of experiencing the principle of "diminishing return" in your life as your addiction runs out of control? The principle of "exponential increase" is, in reality, the pathway out and is the core result of giving away what you so freely received. The self-centered life will continue to sink, but the person who finds the ability to put other's needs at a higher priority than their own, will find buoyancy.

Decide how much increase you want and adjust yourself accordingly!

This inventory becomes the place of a single vision for your life in sobriety. It will provide clarity and undivided focus. It will move you into a posture of vision and push out the division. A clear vision of recovery means it does not matter what anybody else thinks, what anyone says or does, I will choose to stay sober.

We strive to be as God-like as we can by living by the principals. Still, we must face that sometimes we will break some rules, but if we admit it, rectify it, and get back in line, we will have ongoing success.

THE HALLELUJAH HORSE:

A cowboy's horse tripped in a hole and broke his leg. So out in the middle of nowhere, the cowboy had to shoot the horse.

He set off walking and came up to a farm. He asked the farmer if he had any horses for sale. He said, "Sorry, I've recently sold all of my horses, except for the one out there in the back, but you won't want that one, he's a strange piece of work".

The cowboy noticed a rather decrepit looking horse, old and skinny looking like he might fall over dead at any time.

But he was desperate and asked, "How much for that horse?"

The farmer said, "You really don't want that horse. I got him from a crooked preacher who sold him to me and then left town. I don't know what that man did to that horse, but the horse ain't right. I'm not sure he ever really was.»

The cowboy, being desperate for a horse, insisted on buying the horse despite the farmers warnings. So the farmer sold him the horse for a dollar. But before the cowboy rode off, the farmer gave the cowboy some final instructions.

The farmer said, "Now I told you this horse isn't right. He won't respond to anything except for two specific phrases. To make him go, you have to say, 'Thank you Jesus!' To make him stop, you say 'Hallelujah!' "Sounds strange, but don't say I didn't warn you".

The cowboy jumped up on the horse, ready to ride off and hollered gitty-up, let's go, gave the horse a little kick, but the horse didn't move. He tried it again, but the horse just stood there. A little louder and a little harder kick, but the horse didn't move.

Remembering what the farmer told him, he shouted, "Thank you, Jesus!" and instantly the horse went from standing dead still to a full gallop, almost knocking cowboy to the ground.

The horse galloped at full speed, running into fences and bushes, jumping over rocks and ditches. The cowboy, regretting his decision and fearing for his life, became aware that he forgot what the phrase was to make the horse stop.

Just then he saw that the horse was heading full-speed off the edge of a high cliff. The cowboy began frantically pulling on the reins, yelling all the religious words he could think of to try and stop the horse.

Suddenly nearing the edge, he remembered the phrase, "HALLELUJAH!!!"

And instantly the horse stopped dead in its tracks. About a foot away from the edge of the cliff.

The cowboy sat there shaking, soaked in sweat and almost in tears. He had never been so close to his own death before. With a sigh of relief, he wiped his forehead, looked up to the heavens and said,

"Thank you, Jesus!"

CHAPTER 3

HONESTY, TRUTH, VERACITY AND LOYALTY

So, let's build on the principle of honesty. An internal awareness of what one is saying or presenting to others is the measure. Is it not just technically correct, but does it represent the reality at hand? Is the perception being offered to the other person correct? The deciding factor comes from an internal mechanism.

It really comes from a personal perception to start with. Do I believe what I'm saying? There are those that, although they are presenting a falsehood and are lying, believe that what they are saying is true. It's impossible to determine if a person is lying, if in their heart they believe they are not. Some can even beat the lie detector test because the answers they are giving are true to them.

I've met many dishonest people, none of them believed this about themselves.

All the convincing in the world may not move them from their false belief. Personal prejudice, experiential observation, and even our worldview, will shape what we consider to be honest or dishonest. Whatever we believe to be true or whatever is presented to us as true, we are impacted in the same way as if it were and without evidence. It feels true so it must be.

It is the essence of all advertisements. If I can convince you that you'll have the whitest teeth, you will buy my toothpaste. This is the best truck on the market; you've got to have it! These jeans will make you look skinny, or younger or sexier. It may or may not be the reality, but it's what we've been convinced of.

Often it is shaped by what one wants to believe, rather than what one should believe. Even in the face of hard evidence that would tell someone what they believe is not correct, often their desire to believe what they want to believe, may override any hard evidence of what they should. There is data and detail and then there are convictions and conclusions. There are things you want so badly to believe that they become real to you.

Let's take for example if you were going to buy a car. You had considered what kind of car you would like, what would be best for your needs, how much you would like to spend, and when you would like to get your car.

I've dealt with many dishonest men. You can always trust a dishonest man to be dishonest - - - honestly.

Upon arrival at the car lot, you find a car that matches the general description of what you had in mind. You drive it and it is everything that you thought it would be. Then you talk to the salesman. Suddenly he explains to you the extra costs that you didn't plan on. Then comes the minimalistic figure that he gives you for your trade in. Suddenly you are looking at thousands above the price you intended to spend.

You proceed, now a bit cautious, but you're not walking away. You see yourself in this car, you know you would look good driving it. It is really what you need for your life. Well, maybe at least what you want. The salesman emphasizes the features; good gas mileage, seats 4 comfortably, just your color. All the things you were thinking. It must be God. No, he is just a good listener. He explains that you could not find a car like this for this price anywhere. He convinces you that you should buy this car today by giving you a "special price" that the manager must approve, that they wouldn't be able to give to anyone else, except family.

The first sign they might be a little shady, is they say trust me.

Suddenly you're believing something that is likely not true, but you choose to believe it because it's what you want. Often, we believe things not because they are true, but because we want them to be true.

A Good Starting Point

So, we have to start with telling no lies. Here is the logical approach to the topic of truth-telling. There are basic reasons we shouldn't lie.

What Lying Does:

1. Lying creates stress in the person telling the lie. This is often picked up by the listener and the uncomfortable tension stops or hampers the communication.
2. Lying produces guilt which devalues the person telling the lic.
3. Lying dishonors the person to whom the lie is told. Lying communicates protecting myself is more important than respecting you.
4. Lying devalues the listener. Lying says, You arc not worth telling the truth to. You are not important enough for me to disclose what is real.

5. Lying produces after itself. There are often gaps in the story being told with lies. Other lies will become necessary to cover the gaps.
6. Lying breaks the relationship. When the truth comes out, the trust that was there is broken. It may never be regained.
7. Lying leaves the wrong impression, causing others to be seen in a questionable light. Wrong responses often follow.

I sponsored a man for many years. At times, he had long periods of sobriety free from alcohol and drugs. His addiction extended into pornography which, for him, created a lot of problems. He would spend money he didn't have on various websites and live chat rooms and like with his chemical addiction, Norm (not his real name) was always chasing the high.

Eventually he bankrupted his company and his marriage. His wife, a beautifully kind woman, stuck with him longer than anyone could imagine. However, the accumulated damage was done, and one day she had enough and she moved on.

After everything was gone, he found his way back to some facsimile of sobriety again. Relapse was often fostered by trouble with physical pain, so pills became the natural go-to for him. He became so accustomed to using the pills that he could carry himself well and it became increasingly difficult to tell if he was high or not. This is similar to what we would call a functional alcoholic. The person who drinks some every day but maintains their job and their family, so no one seems the wiser. I would add that this type of addict is among the most deceived and dishonest.

The challenge that I really encountered was this; I could never tell whether Norm was being honest with me or not. Some days I'd be sure he was doing wonderfully, saying all the right things and presenting himself to be progressing. This was only to find out later that he was back in some of his old addictive behaviors.

Toward the end of this, during his last bout, I could no longer tell if he was on the pills or not. One day I was in conversation with him, talking recovery and even spiritual matters. The next day I got a call that he had overdosed on heroin laced with fentanyl. In and out of treatment over and over, it became mind-boggling to me. Not the first of this type, but among the most severe.

Let them fail, so they can survive and maybe even grow up.

My conclusion was that I could not help this man. Unless I can live outside of their lies and deception, I cannot assist anyone in recovery from addiction. I could no longer say with any certainty if he was being honest about anything. What's more, when he was telling the verifiable truth, it was often a mask to cover a greater deception. Ultimately, I referred him to another man, Ivan, who I had helped along the way and who had a reputation for effectively helping people through the steps of recovery.

He became willing to work with our man through the step process. However, it was not long until the new sponsor could not tell whether Norm was lying either. The day came when I got the dreaded phone call, like so many before, that Norm had overdosed.

It was my observation and conclusion that Norm wanted my friendship and not my assistance with addiction recovery. He was chasing what I had learned but not what I had earned. Looking for reputation, not restoration. I also concluded that I might be the one thing that was keeping him active in his addiction.

As long as the person, wallowing in addiction and deception on this level, has what appears to be an out, they will not give up. So, similar to what is done with a family in an intervention, I distanced myself from the relationship. Not that I would not be connected at all, but quite obviously I needed to separate myself from Norm.

All the years that I tried to bring assistance, certainly should have planted seeds of sobriety, but ultimately, I became more of a support to the chaos than the recovery. Simply because I could no longer find the divide in Norm between the truth and a lie.

As a final note to this story, rescuing someone who continues to make poor choices is not called love, it's called enabling. Stop enabling and refuse to be a safety net. Let them fall so they can grow up.

Honesty is based on truth. If that which I embrace as truth, is not truth, then what I present as honest is not honest at all. My honesty comes from embracing truth. In the following story, was not being totally honest justified?

To my wife, it was just a license plate. For me, it was a Marine Corps treasure. To me, the license plate was a statement that I had finally defeated the internal shame associated with giving up my military career. Sounds silly I know, but sometimes there are things that appear foolish to one person but carry great meaning to another.

The plate is now on her car and in reality, hers. At least I will get to see it. Soon she adds the Oregon based college team, "the Mighty Ducks" plastic license plate frame which covers part of the plate. This was a purchase made from feeling a connection to the place where she grew up. For her, it was just a license plate and a plastic frame just for fun. For me, it held a deep meaning.

Well I didn't say anything. I just let it go. It passed and I have the Marine Corps license plate back on my truck. I was not really being honest with how I felt but sometimes we choose to let things slide for the greater good. So, was I living a lie or was it just not that important? On a matter so small, should we always declare what we feel or is there a time we should let truth take a second place?

Here is my conclusion: It is a slippery slope to not be honest. Why? Because lying produces after itself. When asked a question by their wife, "Do you like this new outfit?", most men would say yes, even if it were not to their liking. Most times not a problem. But what do you do when she builds an entire wardrobe with that outfit being the main theme?

Now she will know the truth about the license plate, when she reads this book.

Expanding on Truth

Truth is factuality, accurateness, authenticity, credibility, and reliability. We have often read "You will know the truth and the truth will set you free". Not just know about the truth but have an intimate working relationship with it. This only comes by repeated life application. The truth will set you free, but you will need to identify the false beliefs that have been holding you hostage.

The truth is that external body of information that we have worked around. The truth moves beyond the simplistic behavioral patterns and acknowledges that there is outside information that needs to be accepted if we are ever to be honest about the behaviors.

When I was in the Marines, they worked to get us emotionally unattached to dates and times and people, so it would not interfere with our training and ultimately our service commitment. They would say, "Every day is a holiday and every meal a feast". I have heard this approach used in recovery meetings as well. No days are important, everyone is equal, so no people are special, etc. I do not believe it is true. If it were, the following would apply.

1. If everything is equally important then nothing is really important.

2. If every day is the same and nothing is special about a day, then there is never a reason to celebrate.
3. If everyone is equally important then you have no really great special people. You will not hold your family as priority.
4. If every event is wonderful and nothing ever stands out, it becomes diminished enjoyment that will need to be adjusted by getting high.
5. There can be no winners because there can be no losers.

This is called the neutralization of emotions. Herein lies the problem with this approach. If I should feel the same about everything, then obviously feelings don't matter.

For someone who struggles with honesty and truth, everything becomes distorted. For the person in this battle, telling lies and telling the truth feels the same. When this becomes the internal justification for their dishonesty, finding truth is impossible. We then live in the vagaries, whims, unpredictable and erratic actions of an addictive lifestyle.

Objective Truth or Subjective Truth

Objective truth is based in reality and not shaped by unrealistic circumstance or opinions. It is a body of information that is presented with a practical, commonsense approach. Truth about addiction is often intentionally distorted by evidence that promotes a cause. Often money or prestige shapes how it is presented.

Many treatment programs will tell you that you will probably relapse, most people who go through treatment do. They have statistical data to support this statement. They don't tell you that they greatly benefit financially from people repeating, going through treatment more than one time.

I know a program that will allow you back as many times as you can come up with the $10,000 for their 28 day stay. There was general knowledge that they would help you get a second mortgage on your home to fund this. When you're out of money, they send you to AA to get help with staying sober. There is lot of information available to study the experts on the subject. Truth is not only presenting the facts but leaving the right impression.

Here are some variations of truth you might consider. What I call - - -

"Dangerous Truth":

Partial Truth: Withholding information to shape the story.

Careless truth: Becoming chronically inaccurate in what you say.

Enhanced Truth: Information added; exaggeration of a story of personal success or what has been accomplished. Creating the "wonderful" it is or the great "I am".

Shaded Truth: Situational shading. Allowing circumstances to shape your statements.

Slander: Lying about another's character or conduct for personal gain or retaliation.

Flattery: Overt or disproportionate compliments. Saying to a person's face what you would never say behind their back.

Gossip: Unnecessary bearing of information that may or may not be true. Saying behind their back what you would never say to their face. True words with false. implications or insinuations. "The Boss is sober today", (insinuating he is not normally sober).

Silence in the face of a lie: This is complicity by passivity. Not speaking up to defend the truth.

Deception that is believed as truth will have the same effect as if it were true. There are actual reasons why people avoid the truth.

- Fear that the truth will have personal negative consequences.
- Fear of the failure that the truth exposes.
- Fear of how others look at me when they discover what is true.
- Fear of change that the truth may bring about.
- Fear of admitting I was wrong, not just in the immediate but often for an extended time.
- Fear of exposing a life built on compounded lies and false persona.
- Fear of being seen as weak, incompetent, unstable or as a failure.

The problem is that you are already seen that way by those who know you best. You may have convinced yourself otherwise, but most have seen your addiction long before you.

The truth about addiction is that there is a lot of information available to study the experts on the subject. Subjective truth rather than objective truth. Subjective truth is technically honest. It is subjective because it is biased and often partisan. It is truth that is shaped by a distorted perspective. It may be technically truth, but the backdrop causes it to look truer than it is.

Purity of the truth is important. If what you're presenting is 99% true and only 1% falsehood, the entire statement is tainted by the 1% false. An example could be chocolate chip cookies. They are made with 99% chocolate chips and 1% cat poop. I guess the entire cookie would be tainted. Wouldn't you think?

Veracity or The Love of Truth

Veracity is a devotion to the truth, the power of conveying or perceiving truth, conformity with truth or fact and accuracy. The truth produces after itself. A person gains truth about any one thing or person and they fall in love with that truth.

Those that are what we consider a fan or sports enthusiast, have a love for all the information that they can gain about their passion, sports. They study their team, they can name their favorite players, the rankings of the team, the history, the coaches and often even the owners.

Not only do they study their favorite team but they study the opposing teams. They learn all about their rivals, those who could beat them, and of course, those they believe they can win against.

They are prepared, at any time, at any place, to talk about their favorite sport; it is their passion. A huge portion of the television airtime for a football game is devoted to this veracity. There is a panel of experts talking about the game, the players and their outcome prognostication, for hours. Before the game, after the game, comparing to other games and players, 24-hour channels devoted to the game. People spend hours listening to talk about what they think will happen. They even have arguments about the game they watched and what did happen.

Everyone sees it differently, but the commonality is their veracity. The love of information is at the core of all their rhetoric. They desire to learn more, to know more and, of course, to watch more games. This is veracity. The love of truth.

Christians have this love of truth for the Bible and God's interaction with mankind, music lovers for their favorite genre, song or artist. For those in recovery from addiction, it becomes the same type of great passion they had for their addiction when they were using. That was all they talked about. It was the center piece of every conversation they had. But now the focus of this passion has changed to staying free from addictions.

Veracity appears necessary in the world of recovery from addiction. Once a person finds the truth it is not enough to just acknowledge it and even believe it. But to fall in love with this truth and reality about one's life becomes the foundation for building a new life. The success in recovery has, as its groundwork, the need for the levels of passion that equal those that our active addiction had. There are some difficult tasks necessary for recovery and building a sober life. The passion is fueled by the veracity of the knowledge of this great miracle.

As we carry this forward into long term sobriety, it becomes the catalyst for energizing our efforts to help others. Nothing I have seen has the wonderful impact on my personal growth, in life and sobriety, then helping others with theirs. Fall in love with the process and fall in love with the message.

A Lesson in Loyalty

Loyalty is adherence to something to which one is bound by a pledge or duty. It is commitment, dedication, devotion, determination to fulfill what one has started and desires to accomplish.

Loyal to the cause, I can say I've not met many real alcoholics or addicts who were not dedicated to their addiction. Willing to give up family, careers, freedoms and rights, and even personal integrity. Willing to go broke, become ostracized and humiliated, so they could continue in their active addiction.

Loyalty is the next step for the person who is trying to break free from the destruction of the obsessive patterns that drive and sustain the lifestyle hell bent on taking you to the bottom. There is a place for loyalty in sobriety that becomes necessary for you to grow into all that you were purposed to be.

Not just in your personal sober life, but in a life committed to helping others. I am loyal to my sobriety. I have found it necessary to limit myself to those things and people that support my life in sobriety. Having observed others who have failed to maintain some appropriate boundaries, who fail in sobriety, I have set up a lifestyle that supports sobriety.

To this I am loyal. It includes having close personal friends who do not drink or use drugs. Not going to places where the primary function is built around getting high or drunk. Remaining available to assist others who are seeking sobriety. I am loyal to attending recovery meetings as an active part of my life.

I have decided in advance to not drink any alcohol or substitute for alcohol. Near beer, non-alcoholic wine, or toasting with no-alcohol champagne. I do not need to try to pretend to be what I am not.

I have decided to be open with any doctor or medical professional about my addiction. Not to accept prescription drugs without close supervision. Not to forget the great miracle that God gave to me called a life of sobriety.

This applies wherever I go. I have been in recovery meetings in almost every state in the USA and in other countries as well. I make attending a meeting a priority part of my travel plans. Is this necessary to stay sober? Probably not. Is it necessary for me to demonstrate my loyalty to God, my family and my fellow travelers in sobriety? For me yes! Happily.

Each principle builds toward the next.

If you are dealing with getting honest, find truth. Honesty is an inside job, an internal choice. Truth is external. It is that which is outside of me, discovered by others and given to me. The truth of the program of recovery, the truth of relationships and the truth of the Bible. All are external to start with. Once I accept truth and give it priority internally, it produces honesty.

Truth will produce honesty.

Veracity will grow honesty.

Loyalty will secure honesty.

Once I live in truth and see the benefits, I will fall in live with the truth. This is veracity. The place where veracity becomes the centerpiece of my thinking, is where loyalty to the subject matter makes it more than a thought. It now becomes a lifetime promise.

The promise to change is not just to others but is an internal promise, broken again and again. The commitment to keep your promises needs to find a priority in your life and needs to be a priority.

First to yourself, your spouse and the kids, then to your boss and perhaps extended family. How about keeping your promises to society? Promises to God, well, maybe that needs to be first. I have found that promises to God are contained in the other promises I make. While this is not a fail proof method, it will become the user-friendly process that always brings you back to the plum line of your moral standard and commitment to your conscience.

Practical Tips to Get Started

1. Practice habitual observance of truth in your word and actions.
2. Conform your life to truth, fact, and accuracy.
3. Devote yourself to the message of truth and hope.
4. Discover the power of perceiving and conveying the truth.

5. Conform every thought to alignment with the truth.
6. Always say something true that will support and liberate others.

I love the silence where I spend time with my thoughts. Few can embrace the silence even for a moment. The rush of tyrannical thoughts bombards the quiet. Thoughts demanding that I do this or think that. Conversations I will never have blast away the stillness. This process begins and ends with your thoughts.

In the silence, I have made friends with my thoughts. The very thoughts that were onetime fierce opponents are now my allies.

**I am at times my own worst enemy,
other times I am my greatest asset.**

Everything involuntary has its cause in what is voluntary. Man has no greater enemy than himself. I am my own worst enemy an I am also my greatest asset. What you choose to believe about addiction is your choice based on what you know. It is up to you to decide if you want to learn more or stay trapped in limited or wrong information.

It's Time to Learn

At the beginning of the book we covered what we believe about addiction. So, what do you know about addictions? What do you know about your addiction? Is what you know founded in reality or is it just what you want to think is true?

What will keep you trapped where you are?

1. Not admitting the real problem.
2. A focus on cultural beliefs and standards. What society says or what you think they say.
3. Negative peer pressure.

4. Reliving mentally what you have lost.
5. Displaced anger, normally towards those trying to help you.
6. Not starting where you are and with what you have.
7. Delayed response to opportunity. Rejecting help because it is not given in the way you think it should be.
8. Believing no matter what I do, it won't make any difference.
9. Your own words.
10. Pride. It blocks people, God, and open doors.
11. Living in darkness. Believing this life is all there is.

A favorite Bible verse of mine out of the Amplified Bible is,

And you will know the Truth, and the Truth will set you free
John 8:32, AMP

The Message version of the Bible says it a little differently.

"If you stick with this, living out what I tell you, you are my disciples for sure. Then you will experience for yourselves the truth, and the truth will free you."
John 8:31-32 MSG

"One fellow said, the truth will set you free,
but first it will make you miserable".

I would add, before the truth can set you free you need to identify the specific false beliefs that are holding you hostage.

A man went to confession.

He said, “Forgive me Father for I have sinned.”

The Priest asked, “How long since your last confession?”

The man replied, “It has been a long time.”

The Priest said, “What was the nature of your sin?”

The man answered, “I stole some wood.”

The Priest asked, “Where did you steal the wood?”

The man replied, “At a lumber yard, where I work.”

The Priest said, “How much wood did you steal?”

The man replied, “Well, enough to add a bedroom to our house, and a shed at my dad’s, and a barn up on my brother’s farm, and a cabin on our property by the lake.”

The Priest said, “Wow, that’s a lot of wood! We will really need to come up with a serious response to such a violation. Tell me, have you ever done a retreat?”

The man replied, “No, honestly I haven’t, but if you can get the plans, I can get the lumber.”

CHAPTER 4

A CLEAR AND PRESENT DANGER

IN 1990 THERE WAS A book by Tom Clancy called "A Clear and Present Danger". In 1994 it was made into a movie. In this story the actor, Harrison Ford, portrays a CIA Analyst, named Jack Ryan. He is drawn into an illegal war fought by the US government against a Colombian drug cartel. The title of the movie was made clear in the plot.

However, the title was used a long time before the movie was made. It came into being in 1919. It was first announced by the U.S. Supreme Court as the "clear-and-present-danger doctrine". It is a freedom of speech doctrine. I am not a legal expert by any means, but in general, it reflected an early standard by which the constitutionality of laws regulating subversive expression were evaluated in light of the First Amendment's guarantee of Freedom of Speech.

"The question in every case is whether the words used are used in such circumstances and are of such a nature as to create a clear and present danger, that they will bring about the substantive evils, that Congress has a right to prevent." (Speech could be punished if so.)

I loved the movie, the title, and the history. So I thought it would be suitable to present "A Clear and Present Danger" in an applicable form that touches your immediate life. This applies to people, both in recovery and not.

There are many current things that would represent this clear and present danger to us.

Communicable diseases are high on everyone's mind these days. This is not new. We have had many cultural level panics. Legionnaires Disease, Ebola, Zika Virus, H1N1, and more recently, I have heard of Zebra cancer. Of course, the most current crisis that has shut everything down is the Corona virus. All of these are clear in their threat and present a widespread danger to society.

The advent of nuclear weapons being developed by aggressive nations is a formidable global threat. The knowledge that this manner of mass destruction is capable of destroying much of the planet in a short time; it is evident and would be instant.

The United States, is now 20 plus, trillion dollars in debt and spending like there is no tomorrow. Out of control career politicians, without a balanced budget, have foolishly mortgaged the future of generations to come.

The order of the day is hyper social correctness and vigilantism to get one's own way. The danger in being so politically correct is that we will be unable to find the truth from all our pretending.

There is a dangerous trend towards a lowered moral standard. What was not acceptable in private is now hailed on public media as entertainment. Values have flown out the window in our entertainment industry and have had a huge impact on the understanding and guidelines of decency and respect. Laugh tracts are played to make smart mouthed kids considered clever.

As for the United States, we are a divided nation on every front. Right to life vs pro-choice. gun-control vs the freedom to bear arms, open borders vs build a wall, same sex marriage or traditional values, all things political with agendas galore divided into angry debates and volatile protests.

Permission is what I allow into my life.

However, there is a clear and present danger that I have not mentioned, which daily poses a threat to your existence and its form is more palpable than all of these. It is called permission.

Permission

Permission is what I allow into my life; this is still my choice. For the recovering addict and alcoholic, this is both critical and perilous.

The standard is that everything is permissible and allowable for those in recovery. Everything but taking the first drink or drug. The problem is that not all things are helpful or even good for us. Everything is allowed for us until we are brought under its power. Just because something is technically legal does not mean that it is spiritually appropriate.

When we do whatever we think we can get away with, we become trapped in our own self-centered whims. Keep in mind that your spiritual condition is your responsibility. In the chapter on Capacity, Discipline and Authenticity, I spoke extensively about the spiritual condition. But let me address the area most important to staying spiritually alive.

Permission, (your permission) suddenly becomes the gateway for the enemy of your soul (your addiction). The enemy, who is waiting, is just standing at the door; representing the wrong behavior, the wrong thinking, the wrong expression, continually asking for permission to enter, always seeking access, ever desiring asylum, and constantly hoping for a place to operate. The secret place that no one is ever allowed to see. The place you keep your secrets.

Mind you, this enemy is not expressing a demand for control. Your addiction is just comfortably coaxing, "I want to join you and be a part of what you do. I will blend in and no one will know. I will be your friend and ally, I can help you through the rough spots. I can stay small and out of sight. You know that together we can avoid bigger pitfalls. You know the things that have really destroyed you. I'll help you not to fall."

More subtle, vastly deceitful, strikingly clever, and cunning, remarkably disguised as power; like steel covered in velvet. With a friendly smile, the enemy is endearing and brings in special moments of comfort to you. Old memories of getting high, having a good night partying, or some old girlfriend that you got crazy with. Sweet memories.

The Conversation

It's a slow fade into acceptance of this wrong. You respond with a rather lazy response, "I'm fine, I can handle it". You think to yourself "I'll be able to handle it". A little at a time, you buy into the idea. You tell yourself, "I can cover it up and look right before others". You should remember you cannot save face and your butt at the same time.

So, you finally grant permission and the enemy comes in. Familiar and comfortable at first, like finding an old friend after many years. But the comfort season won't last long. The just one won't hurt, becomes the I can stop, but I'm having too much fun. Then how quickly it all begins to unravel again. Once you start the cycle, it seems impossible to stop again.

Then the negative consequences begin. In the end, you will find yourself bewildered and baffled at the terrible impact. These horrific results are met swiftly and gingerly and are countered with, "I'm still here for you. We got through that one together. Was it as good as I promised? It was really good for me. Next time it will be even better." You opened the door and you gave permission, the enemy slipped silently in and you are trapped again.

This is your calamity, your dilemma, your destruction; shrewdly met with the enemy's deep consolation in the form of instant gratification. Quickly he speaks, "Listen, when your friends and family call you out on this, just deny your responsibility; when they don't understand, know that I am here for you. I will always be here to make you feel better".

"Come with me my friend, let's slip off together and wipe the world away. Just for a little while. No one will know. Remember I'll hide well and blend in. You and me together, it's like magic, that's what the others don't understand. You're different, you're unique, you're one of a kind. What we have is special."

I have noticed that the subtle whisper of temptation is a clearer sound than the strongest voice of responsibility.

Oh, the enemy's promise is so deep, rich, and engaging. The very thought of the possibility of an encounter produces instant excitement and anticipated ecstasy. No discussion of the reality that is or the new level of low you will find as you hit bottom again. There is just the promise of a little relief, a new day that will be found as soon as you feel a little better.

He says "Can I have permission to make you feel better? I promise I'll stay out of sight and no one will ever know."

Damn this enemy of my soul. Extricating himself from the damage and pain. Always promising, always gentle, never judging, just smiling, offering, and assuring. Always imploring and alluring. Always loving and kind. Always clear and visible but ever disguised as good and an answer. Always present and always dangerous.

Always just a thought away. Asking once again, "Permission to proceed - - ?"

Your clear and present danger which daily poses a threat to your existence in its form is disguised as a choice. However, it is not a choice in the end, it is called permission. Your choice ends when permission is granted.

At times, we acquiesce; "we accept the enticement reluctantly, but without any resistance or real protest." With ambivalence, we yield. "Permission granted". You can choose the behavior, but you cannot choose the consequence.

Then comes the remorse. That sense of uncertainty which clouds the morning after. That feeling of impending doom, bewilderment and unexplainable uncertainty. Our confidence takes the first hit. We lose all sense of determination and certainty.

The choice takes its toll with fear and confusion. Our conversations are cleverly designed to mask our state of discomfort and dis-ease. We are like a tired swimmer paddling hard to the find the shore. We reach out to our comfort food, television, and other mindless activity and, of course, sleep. These are the inviting escapes and hopefully will be the antidote to our upended emotional and mental state.

Looking at Temptations

We are more comfortable with old problems than new solutions. The real challenge with this is old problems come replete with stress. The old problems become increasingly heavy the longer we carry them. Not always because of stressors does the problem increase. It is the mental torment that you are unable to fix it, becomes apparent. The weight of being held back by it, the mental tiredness that comes from having to think about it, and even the sense of guilt and failure, makes it seem heavier.

Many times, new stress of a much larger scale feels lighter to carry. This is because of the variable called the solvability factor. So, we tolerate the same addiction challenges over and over. Mostly because we are not comfortable with the options available to bring a resolution. So we stay where we are and give permission to the things that are destructive.

So, is the clear and present danger permission? Yes, that and more. This short list is at the core of both the old problems and the new temptations.

- Permission: What I allow in. This is still my choice.
- Proclamation: What I vocalize. Speaking something gives it power.
- Perception: What I focus on. What we become follows what we think.
- Predicate: What I believe forms what I think and what I say.
- Provision: What I make happen for others, both good and bad, will come back to me. We reap what we sow.

This all begins with what I choose to give access. We tend to give permission to those things that are tempting to us. This is what I call pre-addiction tendency's. In our memory of past addictive behaviors and episodes, there remains an unintentional and often spontaneous recall. A remembrance of something good or pleasurable from our former life.

As much as we try to prevent it from developing into a fantasy, there are both mental and physical reactions that occur. We will hear, see, or remember something that becomes the inducement. This is sufficient incentive to activate and arouse desire. It is of no harm unless we give it permission to remain.

The passive desire that we allow to become active in our thoughts, by passive permission, of our own choice, afterwards takes its place and often remains with us against our will. This is how an otherwise innocent thought becomes a temptation and perhaps even a craving.

Subconsciously, we have a vulnerability and affection for the causes of involuntary thoughts, and that is why they come. In the case of voluntary thoughts, we clearly have a desire, a place of weakness, not only for the immediate passion, but also for the people, places, and things that they represent.

The reason we allow the involuntary thoughts to remain and linger for a while is that we have a subconscious attachment to them. If we did not have such a connection or bond, we would dismiss the thought with an urgent expedience.

If the recall included all of the negative consequences, the temptation would lose its power immediately. But the attachment, which is indicative of the pre-addiction tendency, causes us to have selective memory recall.

So temptation for the addicted is just like temptation for anyone else. The exception is that addicts have a greater inclination to escape the present and find a way to feel better.

Temptation Includes:

1. **Promise of pleasure:** Of course, without this promise, temptation would not have it allure. Addiction has a powerful characteristic of being seductive. It is what is commonly known as "romancing the high". The euphoric recall from memories of the last time you experienced it. Similar to that of sexual desires, the mental imagery affects the person both physically and emotionally.
2. **Personal benefit:** There are always the recurring thoughts of what there is to be gained from giving

into these imaginations. The person tempted to rob a grocery store or a bank has an obvious personal dividend. But what about the person tempted to gossip or tell a minor falsehood?What is the measure of individual gain? The enticement comes in a subtle form of how it makes the teller of the story feel somewhat superior.

3. **Participation without consequence:** The promise of pleasure and personal gain is often the great attraction. It is buffered for most people by a clear understanding of the consequences. The deceptive nature of temptation is that it tends toward a guarantee, a promise or, at least, the option of not having to suffer reprisal. For the addict, this is in their thoughts every time they use. It becomes an internal dulling mantra that is easily ignored. The cost for this behavior is often not sufficient to overcome the craving for alcohol or drugs. Divine help is necessary.
4. **Biological, mental, emotional, spiritual impact:** Every part of your being is engaged in the process of temptation. For true temptation will demand that no part is left out. The all-encompassing impact of temptation is that every part of your being is touched at one time. Should a part not be stirred or disturbed, that part would automatically begin to resist. The wholeness of your self is the best preemptive resistance you can have against temptation.
5. **Always a way of escape:** With every temptation, there is a way out.

There is that moment of hesitation when rational thoughts surface. A strong feeling that I should stop now. A churning in your stomach that something is wrong. Of course, there is a spiritual prompting that this is a wrong choice. It is so easy to ignore the first thought. However, the longer you delay in offering resistance, the less likely it is that you will succeed in thwarting the temptation.

There are warning signs all along the path— DANGER—STOP—TURN AROUND! We have heard the testimony of others which should tell us that we don't have to repeat their mistakes. Our story is the same as theirs. The only difference is that we know at the beginning what they found out at the end. Despite the warnings, both internal and external, we are just as capable of falling victim to temptation as they were.

We should not be so cocky and overtly self-confident. No one is excluded from the battle found with temptation. You're not exempt now, nor will you ever be. You could fall flat on your face as easily as anyone else. Forget about thinking you are too spiritual. Discard the over self-confidence. It will not help you.

Some temptations come to productive, powerful people, but all temptations seek out the passive and the proud.

Build your relationship with the Lord and get filled up. Filled up with knowledge, emotional health, and mental alertness. Get physically in shape and spiritually built up. Get full of recovery. I have discovered my full fights for me. At least it provides a place that I can resist more effectively.

No temptation or trial will ever come your way that is beyond what other people have faced. All you need to remember is that God will never let you down. God will never let you be pushed past your limit. God will always be there to help you come through it.

The clear and present danger is your permission. Nothing happens without your permission. Though it appears that this matter is somewhat involuntary. But you can be sure that it is rooted in something more voluntary than not. We have seen that with temptation, we have no greater enemy than ourselves. We are usually aware of what it is that we can or cannot do. However, when temptation comes, it will show us just who we are. It is no longer a matter of can or cannot, but will or will not.

Every time we resist any temptation, we gain the strength of that temptation. Your enemy will downplay small temptations. This sets the stage to bring us to into greater ones.

This is where the importance of your story comes into play. We find the freedom to believe when we recall past battles and victories. In sharing our story we eliminate faulty beliefs about God, our memories, our imaginations, and passions.

- Behaviors reveal motives
- Religion masks weaknesses

- Consequences expose violations
- Desires cover inappropriateness

- Truth examines our life
- Ideology excuses failures

Our remembering takes us out of living in the past when we can capture it and openly share what used to be our dark secrets. Living in the past opens the door for shame. Recycled shame produces after its kind. Living in the future creates fear and apprehension. The fear of failing again should one not live perfectly.

Our story puts us into today. Yesterday I was weak and failing. Tomorrow holds with it much uncertainty. But today I can be empowered. I can escape every temptation through patience and prayer.

Patience and prayer are effective and active only in the present. If you oppose temptation without these, it will only attack you more strongly.

Resisting is in the Now:

1. We stop fighting anyone and anything.
2. We adopt a set of moral guidelines to better govern our lives.
3. We enter prayer, both individually and collectively.
4. We embrace caring for others as a life staple.
5. We refrain from speaking evil of anyone at any time.
6. We prefer the desires of others over ours.
7. We demonstrate the adoption of a group of principles that are spiritual in nature.
8. We are now part of something greater than ourselves.
9. We have gained the moral advantage.

"Do not let anyone under pressure give in to evil by saying, "God is trying to trip me up." God is impervious to evil and puts evil in no one's way. The temptation to give in to evil comes from us and only us. We have no one to blame but the leering, seducing flare-up of our own lust."

James 1:13-14 MSG

WHO'S OBSESSING?

A man visits a psychiatrist.

The doctor says, "How can I help you?"

The man replies, "I think I am obsessed with sex. Can you help me?"

The doctor agrees to examine him and begins by showing him various drawings.

First, the doctor draws a circle, and ask the man, "What do you see?"

The man says, "One man having sex."

The doctor then draws a triangle. Then he shows the man the drawing and says to the man, "What do you see?"

The man replies, "Two women and one man having sex."

Next the doctor draws a square and asks the man to identify it.

The man responds, "Four people having sex!"

The doctor puts the drawings away and says,

"I agree. You do seem to have an obsession with sex."

The man replies, "ME???

YOU'RE the one who's drawing all the dirty pictures!"

CHAPTER 5

THE PROGRESSION OF OBSESSION

OVER THE MANY YEARS I have worked with people and addictions, one of the common traits, I have seen most often is obsessive thinking. So I thought it would be important to dedicate one chapter to obsessive planning or thinking, in what I referred to as the "Progression of Obsession". I will try to give an understandable explanation of how i seen it impact those trying to get sober.

There are four basic parts to this progression:

1. Obsessive planning
2. The narrowness of opportunity
3. The illusion of control
4. Diminished time continuum value

The progression of obsession starts with a thought. Just a simple, seemingly innocent, thought. Now for some people, this certain thought would pass without a moment's hesitation. Just a fleeting thought of no necessary significance. We have thousands of thoughts every day. Estimates range from 60,000 to 80,000 a day.

This number is not just your conscious thoughts. Just posting on

Facebook is a long series of thoughts, including typing and spelling the words - during which you might note a lawnmower noise outside, tell Siri to turn down the song that was playing, check the time, and consider who will like your post. There is, of course, all the subconscious thoughts, memory, feelings, and stressors. It could be that 70,000 is a very conservative number compared to the possible number of thoughts a person can have each day. This means we have multiple thoughts every minute of every day.

Then comes a thought that gets our attention. In some cases, our undivided focus. An idea that for most would not even land. There it is recurring a second and third and hundredth time. Not just for a moment but it has moved in. We think of another thought to displace the intruding thought. There, I have solved it. The rogue thought is gone. Nope, now it's back. Really? I don't want to think about it. We discover that not wanting to think about it, is thinking about it.

It could be dreading a visit to the dentist; an unpaid bill with no resources to cover it or the rehearsal of an emotionally disruptive episode in your day. Playing over and over.

Recently, I stopped off at a local Publix grocery store to buy a package of cookies for a meeting I was heading to. I had just finished a long overdue bank transaction clearing an old mortgage and was enjoying the beautiful cool Florida weather. Things were good.

I backed my large pickup into a great parking spot and stopped when the rear beeper went off so I wouldn't hit the pole behind me. When I got out, I noted I was hanging out in the street a little farther than I thought. A passing woman said to me, "I hope you're not going to leave that hanging out in the street!" I smiled and jokingly replied, "Well, maybe I will". She yelled, "I hope someone hits it and smashes it!".

I responded, this time not with a smile, "Well, thank you!" She, now standing in the middle of the parking lot with her shopping cart, began to give me a piece of her mind. (I was now convinced she really needed all of her mind she could keep).

I was getting back into my truck to move it back as she was going on and on, when out of nowhere, without a thought I told her to shut up, not politely either. She continued her rant, calling me out, "Come on", she said, as if she wanted to fight it out right there in the parking lot.

I replied, "Move along - - - - -!" (I called her a name, not obscene, but a rude name). She left, and I backed up the truck. Two other ladies behind me who were watching, were laughing at the incident.

I went into the store feeling like an idiot. I don't normally argue with strangers and never call people names. I rehearsed the situation, over and over, for the rest of the day. That was last week. Apparently, I'm still having the thoughts, as I'm now writing about the episode.

So, why does one thought get stuck and overstay its welcome? We would like to change something that has passed or control that which has not happened yet. Remorse for the past and fear of the future could, in a simple way, explain an obsessive thought.

But, of course, a thought is just a thought. It needs no further action or explanation. Just a lone independent thought hanging around. No, not normally. If it remained a singular thought it would be self-eliminating. So, what happens when a simple, singular, independent, stand-alone thought becomes more?

When thoughts remain in the conscious mind, they begin to expand while simultaneously connecting with other thoughts. They will become something together that seems to take on a life of its own. An expanded thought often attaches itself to an emotion. The feeling and thought combine into an opinion. Opinions become judgements, determining right and wrong. Mental judgements promote the idea of taking an action. So, out of a single thought, an entire mental plan is birthed.

Obsessive Planning

What we obsess about determines our direction. Our level of obsession determines our momentum. One is where we are going, the other is how fast we are going there. We rehearse in our mind the thought in context with the real or imagined episode. We then begin to build plots, imagining what could happen. Commonly we play out the "he said, she said" scenario. If it is a past episode, we rehearse what we could have said, should have said or would have done. If it is a future episode we imagine what it will be like, who will say what, and what the outcome will be.

The first part of this is what we obsess about. This is the direction we are going. It can be good or bad, depending on our perspective. So I will start with the positive side of obsessive thinking. History is replete with obsessive thinkers. It seems a person who accomplishes anything worthwhile needs to stay focused. Keeping that one thought or goal in mind, no matter what else happens or what anyone says to the contrary.

Most successful people have a long history of failing before they ever achieve the success they are known for. I have listed a few of my favorites, but the list could go on and on.

1. Colonel Harland Sanders was the founder of Kentucky Fried Chicken (KFC) restaurants. At the age of sixty-five, and broke with a lifetime of failure, he set out to sell his franchise chicken model. 1,009 restaurants rejected him before one accepted his offer.
2. Thomas Edison is by far one of the most famous inventors in history. He holds 1,093 patents to his name. However, when attempting to invent a

commercially-viable electric lightbulb, he failed 1000 times. His teachers said he was "too stupid to learn anything."

3. Henry Ford is the father of the automobile and quite possibly one of the most famous industrialists to have ever lived. He went broke multiple times before he succeeded.
4. The hit movie and TV series M*A*S*H was turned down by over 20 publishers, but Richard Hooker the creator, didn't give up.
5. New York City store, Macy's, failed seven times before R. H. Macy found success.
6. The Beatles have sold over 1.6 billion albums and counting. However, on New Year's Eve in 1961, when they drove in a snowstorm to audition at Decca Recording Studios, they were rejected.
7. The founder of Woolworth's, F. W. Woolworth, was told by his employer that he could not wait on customers, because he didn't have enough sense.
8. The famous Dr. Seuss's first book, To Think That I Saw It on Mulberry Street, was rejected 27 times before it was published.
9. At 95 years old, one of the most accomplished cellists that ever played was still practicing six hours a day. When asked why, Mr. Casals said, "Because I think I'm making progress."
10. Walt Disney created the Walt Disney Company after he faced many failures. His first company, Laugh-O-Gram, went bankrupt. It wasn't until 5 years later and plenty of heartache, that he created Mickey Mouse and built the empire it is today.

So, what did these people have in common? They were obsessive thinkers. They did not let go of the plan, they stayed focused in spite of how it looked or what the odds were.

I cannot speak for any of them beyond the obvious that they were in some form obsessed with their purpose and plan. There are those who I have met who have a similar trait which I refer to as "Obsessive Progressives". They may not have achieved any large measure of success but are the obsessive thinkers among us. It seems that obsessive thinking is necessary for them to move forward, in even the smaller tasks.

This obsessive thinking produces positive results but may tend to be frustrating to those around them. These obsessive progressives find it necessary to have a singular focus in order to accomplish any kind of project. It would seem as though they lack the capability for doing the simplest form of a task without constantly and intently focusing on it. They are not easily distracted and locked to a thought they plow forward.

A good example of this is the person who is getting ready to make a public presentation or a big speech. The preparation time includes writing notes, researching ideas on the subject and even exploring the culture of the audience, and of course for most, at least the smart ones, prayer.

However, the greatest amount of time is often spent in mental review obsessing on how it will sound, how the audience will respond and even what the applause will sound like at the end. The speaker wants to do a good job of informing, inspiring and even entertaining.

This obsessive thinking allows the progressive development of the speech. The problem is when it's taken to the extreme. Now, it is no longer obsessing on the idea of doing well, the event becomes overwhelming. That which was a healthy, insistent focus, now becomes worry, fear and undue concern about everything and anything.

The abnormal amount of time we spend thinking about anything, becomes an accurate predictor of where we are headed.

This leads us to the negative side of obsessive thinking. Not only can it produce excessive worry and unrealistic fears, it can actually stop us from making any form of progress. The abnormal amount of time we spend thinking about anything, becomes an accurate predictor of where we are headed. If the thinking is negative, it will either take the person into unproductive, sometimes dangerous action, or cause them to become paralyzed in the thought.

We see this when romantic relationships end or marriages are dissolved in divorce. If one of the parties will not or cannot let go, they can easily become caught up in the obsessive thinking trap. Reviewing over and over what they could have done, should have done or maybe can still do, to keep the other person in the relationship.

While their former partner has moved on, they remain trapped in their thoughts. The obsession often becomes so destructive that legal measures are taken to get the person to stop.

In addiction, the same principle applies. An obsession for alcohol or drugs, or food, or gambling becomes the central theme to everything in life. It is all that the addicted person thinks about. There are other parts to life for them, but no plans exist without the inclusion of their drug of choice.

Options for a party, attendance at a sporting event, hobbies like fishing or hunting, even something simple like going out to dinner, always makes room for the addiction. The rest of the plan always revolves around it.

The Narrowness of Opportunity

The longer we obsess on one thing, the less likely it is that we can effectively process other options. This imbalance will affect every part of the person's life and well-being.

Obsessiveness makes us feel "not ok". When a person does not feel ok, selfish behaviors will always follow. This is particularly noted in the addictive personality since everything in the addict's life revolves around self.

The self-centered, self-seeking, out of control self-will is the crux of the problem. In this obsessive condition, they will struggle to comprehend anything about the world outside themself. They may also find it difficult to accurately or rationally assess what's happening inside of themselves. A person in this state would make a terrible detective. They can only investigate one thing and will inadvertently ignore what is obvious to others.

Let's use the case of a person trying to get employment. To be successful at securing a position, you need a company that is hiring in a role you are qualified for, an application, an appointment to interview, and the invitation to be employed with the company. Not every application results in an interview and not every interview produces a job.

So, our candidate fills out an application, someone casually looks at it and says, "We will call you". They feel good about this company and the job so they wait for the call. Confident they will be hired, they don't fill out more applications or engage in any further search. They become obsessed with the thought that this job is a sure thing; it is all they can think of for employment. This obsessive thought blocks out all other possibilities. It has narrowed everything available down to one thing.

People do this with a first date. So enthralled with one person, they forget there are lots of options. The stronger the obsession, the less they can see any alternative. This applies to people buying a car or a home. They become so emotionally attached that they don't even consider all of the many options available.

The Illusion of Control

If I just think about it long enough, rehearse it often enough, or focus hard enough, I can control what the outcome will be. Our obsession may be positive or negative. It is often running to something or away from something, real or imagined, sometimes both. Obsession, good or bad when taken to the extreme, will have negative fallout. However, the idea that I can control what is happening is at the core of every obsessive person.

It seems to the obsessed that if I am to think about this matter continuously, I will then gain control over the matter. The process of rehearsing the details, the good and bad, the likely and the unlikely, seems to give a false sense of the influence that I am certain to have. It is feasible that I will mentally predict an outcome that will favor me and have the desired conclusion I am hoping for.

The thoughts formulated give a false sense of empowerment. The longer I rehearse the scenario, the more I feel that I am in control. This is compounded when I have made it a matter of praying what it is that I desire. Believing that God will automatically give a yes answer to my prayers, enhances the illusion that I am in control.

I have seen that, for many, the walls of denial are built with this false image and misconception. It often evolves into delusional thinking that involves how others will respond and what choices they will make. I have seen many tragic endings that have stemmed from this faulty thought process.

Positive outcomes are often displaced by the illusion the person has of controlling the outcome. One story is of a woman infatuated with a nationally known, high level preacher. He was immensely popular in his day and was a sought after speaker globally.

The woman was so obsessed by her plans to marry this man that she began to write to him. Although he did not respond for some time, eventually he responded to her with an emphatic letter asking her to stop. However, her mental processes told her that she would marry this man. She told her friends, her pastor and anyone else who would listen to her plans. She made it sound as though the minister was on board with the entire matter.

Unable to make any real progress, her obsessive thinking would not allow her to consider any other option except this delusion of marriage to someone to whom she had never been introduced.

Eventually she was so convinced of her control of the situation, she flew to the city where he was ministering. She dressed herself in a wedding gown and showed up unannounced the large auditorium where he was speaking. With thousands in attendance, she strolled down the aisle to marry the minister. Suffice it to say, she was met with an able and compassionate security team who escorted her from the place.

The illusion of control will cause people to wait for jobs that they have applied for, money to come from the lotto and even their knight in shining armor to ride in. Many real opportunities have been totally missed in this process.

Diminished Time Continuum Value

The amount of time we spend on an obsession is our time continuum. The longer we obsess, the more the time spent loses its value. There comes a point where in normal circumstances, we would never devote the volume of time to something so unproductive. However, the obsession takes away the normalcy of perspective.

Consider the alcoholic sitting at the bar. Hours, days, even years spent with very little thought of the value of the time he has wasted. Obsessed with his drinking, he squanders away his time. Time better spent doing almost anything else. Time with his wife, time with his children, gone. Time to make additional income instead of spending what little money he has.

Time with a hobby, time for self-development, exercise, reading, and traveling. All dissipated and used up by nothing other than the great obsession, his drink. Obsessions always come with a natural byproduct of diminishing some other area of your life. Obsessions can add energy in a positive way to create focus or momentum or they can take our energy away from what would be productive. Obsession will either produce success or chaos.

The amount of time that we devote to a particular project, hobby or undertaking is a time continuum. The time we spend extends out from other activities without a clear delineation.

In essence, it reveals that our hobby or activity will begin to blend itself into what we would normally spend our time doing or devoting our time to. This is particularly true when it comes to addiction. It infiltrates and consumes time that otherwise would be naturally devoted to normal activities. The time that is spent and given exclusively to one matter will strip time away that would be better spent elsewhere.

We see this with the person taking a longer lunch so they can drink; leaving work early and heading to the bar, drinking on the job, and even skipping work to take off on a bender. The time continuum becomes reduced by the interloper. The thief takes from everyone who should be receiving the benefit and deserving of the time. The value of how and where we apply our time and effort is lost in the obsession.

Obsession will either produce success or chaos.

The same idea applies to financial matters. An obsessive drinker will have a diminished financial continuum as well. It slowly erodes any extra money and robs him of all future potential. It will not only take the future, but the current needs and obligations are also frequently neglected.

A diminished emotional continuum is also a major victim. The time away from family and relationships robs them of emotional stability. Slowly it pilfers our affection for our loved ones and defrauds them of the love and attention they deserve. The same displacement of affection and passion applies to our work and even to our relationship with God.

So our diminished time continuum is mostly reflected in and seen by the lack of value we put on each moment we waste. Minutes become hours that without much notice to the person caught in his obsessive planning, accumulate into days, then weeks and ultimately years. The shift is subtle, and it is a slow fade. When a person looks back over their life, what they will see first and foremost is the amount of time that they've wasted.

Interestingly, many do not adjust their time application and, although they are now sober, they continue to treat time as an endless commodity. Rather than reprioritize and place their family, work, and relationship with God as the new normal, they redirect their time and affection to other selfish activities.

Until the recovery process is entered into and the healing begins, the obsessive plans and thinking will continue. To the onlooker, the person appears to have just moved from one bad behavior to another. It is like changing seats on the Titanic, eventually it won't really matter.

Embracing the process of recovery and finding relief from the brokenness is necessary. You cannot replace time. You cannot change the beginning, but you can start now and change the ending.

Your now is not your forever.

So let's review the idea. There are four basic parts to the Progression of Obsession.

1. **Obsessive planning,** it is believing that thinking about one thing over and over will cause it to change.
2. **The narrowness of opportunity,** is losing the ability to consider other viable options do to obsessive thinking.
3. **The illusion of control,** is the belief that we control the outcomes by our repetitive thoughts.
4. **Diminished time continuum value,** is the lost ability to measure the amount of time wasted on that which is unproductive.

Because of his stupidity and clumsiness, Kyle's teacher was always yelling at him, "You're driving me crazy.»

One day Kyle's mama came to school to check on how he was doing.

The teacher told his mama honestly that her son was simply a disaster, getting very low marks, and that she had never seen such a stupid boy in her entire teaching career.

The mom was so shocked at the feedback that she withdrew her son from school and moved out of Detroit, relocating to Cleveland.

Twenty-Five years later, this same teacher was diagnosed with an almost incurable cardiac disease. All the doctors strongly advised her to have open heart surgery, which only one surgeon at the Cleveland Clinic could perform. Left with no other options, the teacher decided to have the operation which was successful.

When she opened her eyes after the surgery, she saw a handsome young doctor smiling down at her. She wanted to thank him, but could not talk. Her face started to turn blue, she raised her hand trying to tell him something but she quickly died.

The doctor was shocked, wondering what went wrong so suddenly. Then he turned around and saw our friend Kyle, a janitor in the Clinic, who had unplugged the life-support equipment in order to connect his vacuum cleaner.

If you thought Kyle had become a heart-surgeon, there is a high likelihood you need this chapter.

CHAPTER 6

ADDICTION DISCURSION

(discursion) (noun) step by step philosophic reasoning, the act of discoursing or reasoning; as from thought to thought. It is the description of feeling, impact or solution"

The Addiction Discursion

This could be called "Inventory Mapping". As we move through the stages of this process, each stage reveals one more level of our personality that has been impacted by our behavior.

The 6 Stages of Inventory Mapping:

1. **Active Addiction**
2. **Addictive Behavior**
3. **Low Self-esteem**
4. **Low Self-worth**
5. **No Self-image**
6. **Shame Based Issues**

Addiction Principles

As we explore the Addiction Discursion, it is duly noted that not all addictions are the same, but all have common characteristics.

These are what I describe as "Addiction Principles". We will see some of these in the various stages of our mapping. They are common in all addictions and manifest in everyone that is addicted, on some level.

A common addiction principle is known as "the craving". I placed this at the front of the list. Most everyone has cravings on some level. A physical, emotional, or even mental desire. A longing that doesn't seem to go away. A common craving people have is for a certain kind of food, such as ice cream, pizza, candy, momma's casserole, or pot roast. (Not so much of a demand for broccoli or beets, but I'm thinking someone, does, somewhere). It is a certain thought that repeats itself and brings with it pleasant thoughts of the reward of the taste or feeling that will be experienced.

This is a normal experience but for those addicted, and it is commonly more intense than it is for the average person. It becomes an obsession that usually progresses into a compulsive action. Left alone, the craving becomes a demand to take some action. This extends to the destructive behaviors seen in the out of control addict or alcoholic.

Once what has been called the "phenomenon of craving" is active, it would seem there is little, if anything, that can be done to stop it. Once the addicted person responds to the craving, unlike a person with normal cravings, the craving only increases and wants more.

Craving comes from the root word crave. Another form of this word crave, is craven. They are similar in root meanings. It is apparently adapted from Old French word "cravent", which means defeated or beaten. It is clear that when the craving is given place, we will be all too soon defeated.

Addiction Principles

> **Confusion and deception** These are found in most people who are battling with addiction. They have

believed their own self-talk for so long that the fantasy world they have created seems to have become their reality. They have centered their communication with others with such dishonesty that they have trouble discerning the truth.

Despair and fear Both are common traits. It is the overwhelming feeling of something wrong, or something missing, which often produces panic. This is coupled with the idea that it will always be this way and I will never have peace or happiness.

Isolation This is a core issue with the addicted. Keeping to myself is an effective way of masking my addiction. Not wanting people to see what you are doing is difficult when you constantly have to cover your tracks. Keeping people away is routine, but an overwhelming loneliness that only the addicted know, is the natural outcome. They need someone to pay attention them without being seen. It is a abstract feeling of being needed without allowing anyone close .

Suspicion of others It is mostly evidenced in an extreme caution. Few people are trusted and actually, no one is completely. This is the byproduct of knowing that you yourself are not to be trusted.

Other addiction principles include wrong priorities and life choices, the inability to stop or control your own will, lost jobs and status, family dysfunction, broken promises, etc. Clearly this is not an exhaustive list, but you can get the idea.

These and many other characteristics of the addictive personality will be seen in the various stages of your inventory. So, let's look at the addiction discursion and map out our inventory.

1. Active addiction:

It should not go without saying that most people today are familiar with active addiction. When it is at its full measure, it is easily identifiable to the average person. But oddly enough, not so much for the person engaged in it. In the legal profession, there is what is called the "rule of the reasonable person". Basically, it describes what the average person would do or behave under a common set of circumstances.

For the person in active addiction, this seems to be an elusive concept. The standard responses coming from this person are anything but reasonable. The presenting life priority is not for the well-being of those around, such as family and friends; it is not for the fulfillment of responsible adult activity, such as paying bills, maintaining health or achieving goals.

It is, rather, the priority of each day to ensure that everything necessary to maintain the addiction is accomplished. I'm not saying that other matters are never taken care of quite the contrary. Often the individual caught in addiction is precise in accomplishing normal life activities, at times out of a guilt reaction to their addictive behavior.

The amount of time given to the addiction, money spent that would be better utilized for other things, and the shame that comes from covering the behavior which "I promised I wouldn't do". The attention given to the parts of life that are important to others, becomes part of the ruse to mask the active addiction. Often large amounts of energy are spent on covering the addiction.

This behavior camouflage increases with usage and the plans often become increasingly elaborate. This extends to the place where they are exposed. It does not mean that they will automatically discontinue the game, but rather that they will work to convince those around them they have changed and are no longer in active addiction.

The second level of addiction masking may include a more intricate plan to cover the addiction. This cat and mouse game will most likely continue until the parties who are negatively impacted separate themselves from the actively addicted or until true recovery is embraced.

Deception toward others stems from layers of self-deception.

All active addiction contains such deception and is in and of itself part of the addiction. This deception toward others stems from layers of self-deception and is rooted deep in the base brokenness of the individual's physical, mental, emotional, and spiritual life.

Actually, the spiritual malady is the principle factor keeping a person in active addiction. The mental confusion, the emotional pain and the physical cravings can all be healed. Once a persons spiritual life is restored or embraced for the first time, the remainder of the person's life can move forward into restoration and permanent recovery.

Active addiction includes other dimensions starting with the universal characteristic called craving. This is an appetite that can never be satisfied. The longing and desire, often for something that seems to be missing; the need to fill the sense of void often described as an empty hollow feeling. It is a longing to feel part of something, the urge to change people, places or things, a lust for what they can't have or a yearning to feel fulfilled with what they do have, a state of non-contentment.

Enough is never enough, to him who enough is too little.

At this point, the addict reaches for the drink or drugs that will fill the empty space for a while. A drug that will numb the pain of displacement. The gambler will launch out on a chase, with a promise of great reward that will fill the void with money, property, and recognition.

The sex addict will grab the pornography and enter a fantasy world for a while. An entire chocolate cake, binge working over the weekend, or burying oneself in the disconnected life of online games. It doesn't matter the addiction, the response to the pain activates reaching for something to fill the void.

So, let's return to the rule of the reasonable man for a moment. The behavior of an active addict makes no sense to a person without addiction. Why, after failure upon failure, would the person repeat the same behavior?

Financial investment people understand this concept as the rule of the prudent man. What money decision seems acceptable? What pays the best dividend? What is a secure way to handle resources?

In this scenario, the person's experience and expertise would vastly affect the choices made. Operating out of logic, factual evidence and the direct or even indirect counsel of those making similar choices, the plan is formulated. A person of less experience would likely make choices that would be less prudent.

This is the reason many who win the lotto end up broke in a short time. Driven by feelings, they are unable to create sound choices to insure long term planning. For the onlooker, the matter appears to be insanity. For the person in the mix, it is exercising what appears to be normal, solid options.

An individual living in active addiction is caught in the deception of normalcy bias. Normalcy bias blinds the person to an extent that they cannot believe the inevitable crisis is going to happen. Remaining in their trap, they continue in behaviors that are clearly destructive. The outcome cannot be anything but disastrous, yet they stay in harm's way. It may be that they have not yet experienced the inevitable calamity that will result from their choices and actions. So, they continue on, oblivious to what is coming. While it is obvious to those looking on, the addict doesn't believe that it will happen to them.

Those that drive while drinking alcohol are convinced that they can drive better, because they are more relaxed. They are sure that they won't get caught, at least this time. Banking on the law of averages, they get behind the wheel and off they go. Most often way past the legal limit, not believing that anything bad will happen. They have practiced this behavior for so long that the idea of disaster is blocked.

The belief that we who are addicted are different from normal people, is called "terminal uniqueness".

They see the police and fear grips their heart, then the officer goes past, and they laugh. "See, I won't get caught". They do not believe that there will be any possibility of an accident. Any injury to themselves or others is not in the equation. They have heard of people getting killed driving under the influence or killing someone else, but it won't be them. They are different. This is referred to as "terminal uniqueness".

When hurricanes are here in Florida, it is amazing the number of people who simply don't move out of the way. Tracking and reporting goes on for days, even weeks. Warnings that it's coming are everywhere. Options to go elsewhere are made available. But many don't believe it will impact them, so they stay put.

Before Katrina, it was predicted that the levees were not going to hold, but tens of thousands stayed. Hurricane Katrina was the largest and third strongest hurricane ever recorded to make landfall in the US. In New Orleans, the levees were designed for a Category 3 hurricane, but Katrina peaked as a Category 5, with winds up to

175 mph. The results was final death toll of 1,836 and 705 people are reported as still missing.

Many who have had the deception of normalcy bias regarding their addiction have paid the ultimate price for their delusion. Every heroin addict who has died was under some delusion that they could beat the odds. Many around them had overdosed, ended up hospitalized or dead. But it won't happen to them.

I have observed a pattern in alcoholics and addicts that reflects this so well. I call it "the one last dance syndrome". For the man who has floated in an out of recovery for many years, this is a familiar scenario. They want recovery and its benefits. They see how this can be possible because so many have made the journey. They have had some periods of sobriety, but never took it seriously. They believe that if they were to actually enter the process, they could beat this thing. It's not that hard. People who have been much worse off have accomplished this.

This time will be different.

So the overly confident man or woman continues to play around the edges. Experiencing some consequences, but always able to come back from it. Now facing serious consequences, they are serious about recovery. No more games. No more broken promises. This time will be different. Convinced that they have made a true commitment, they head back to meetings. They pick up the language, participate in the groups, and even call other members.

The accolades begin. To any onlooker, it appears that this time they have it. And who knows, maybe they do. But let's not sound the trumpets too soon. There are a lot of temptations to endure and many hurtles to get over before the person is out of the woods. At any juncture, the person could slide off into a detour. There is the matter of the last dance stuck in their mind. The moment of maybe, the pause of perhaps, the insidious what if, still lingers.

They think that they are different. They are smarter than the average person. They're unique, unlike those other addicts, they have been able to quit before. What about one last dance before hanging it up, this time for good! Quickly, they dismiss the thought, but not completely. They reserve the option to review the concept at a later time. After all, someone, somewhere must have beaten the odds, so they certainly can pull it off. This is an illusion of control. But how did they get to this place?

2. Addictive Behaviors:

The next level in our addiction discursion is patterned after the active addiction level. However, at this point, the person is no longer trying to cover their drinking, or using the drug of choice; they have stopped using any mind altering substance. They are however still acting out in destructive behavior. Actually, this level they seems to be equally confused as our "reasonable man" onlooker. The addiction is gone, so why are you still lying? What about the out of control anger? You seem afraid of everything, why?

It has been observed that, from the time a person is completely detoxed from alcohol and drugs until the window of about 90 days sober, give or take a few, the addictive behaviors increase. This is commonly referred to as "Post-Acute Withdrawal Syndrome". Much has been written about the subject of PAWS, and an expanded study is found in the book "What You Need to Know" by Terence T. Gorski.

These addictive behaviors come from a combination of physical, mental, emotional, and spiritual adjustments. Possible causes are damage to the nervous system caused by alcohol or drugs and the stress that comes from living with life without drugs or alcohol.

Many people who become addicted, particularly those who abuse substances, often have emotional challenges before becoming addicted. Often we see the substance abuse escalates from trying to self-medicate their symptoms. During their active addiction, the emotional challenges sometimes become even more prominent. The drugs or alcohol, food or other escapes actually block their true feelings. Once the substance abuse has ended, processing emotions becomes increasingly difficult. Now, with nothing to block how they feel, they are more prone to overreacting to situations which normally would be dealt with easily.

Often explosive, driven by core issues of anger and fear, they become more intense and seem impossible to please or interact with. When confronted, they may escalate or completely shut down and feel nothing. Often, they enter the flight, fight or freeze mode of coping with life or perhaps not coping with life is a better description. Memory challenges, disrupted sleep patterns, moodiness, clumsiness, and diminished coordination are often experienced in this stage of addictive behavioral adjustment.

The inability to have a proper diet affects all of these. This comes from a lifetime of bad eating habits, a lack of knowledge about the nutritional needs of your body, easily accessibility to fast foods and for some, food addiction. Many times, the craving for real nutrition, not just empty calorie foods, is mistaken for the craving associated with drugs, alcohol, or other addictions.

Our bodies signal a need and we mask it with unsuitable alternatives. Most addictive types fail in both nutrition and exercise. Taking care of your body produces clear dividends. Better sleep, more energy, clear thinking, and of course, an improved emotional life can follow.

The addictive behavior stage of recovery is commonly known as a “dry drunk”. All the behaviors of a person in active drinking or drug use, but without the substances to get you high. The anticipated outcome is either the person will go back to active addiction or seek relief with some manner of outside help.

Low Self-esteem:

Low self-esteem develops from not being able to contribute and be productive. It is how one sees what they do, their place in life. It's their perceived inability to contribute to life; a focus on all the mistakes they've made which creates a pattern of negative self-talk. This self-centered focus fosters an internal narrative of self-accusation, self-denunciation, and censure. It results in a lack of caring for others, failure in solving life problems and not being motivated, all of which are evidence of low self-esteem and the harbinger of things to come.

These are not simply indicators, but actually tend to foster an expanded possibility of low self-esteem. Like being caught in an ever-tightening vortex, a downward spiral happens. The unprovoked embarrassment, a sense of impending doom (with or without a corresponding stimulus), small menial tasks often seem overwhelming, and a general sense of being uncomfortable.

There is often a fear of failure that blocks taking on even small assignments, coupled with a marked inability to deal with routine life problems, such as financial stress stemming from poor work routines, unbalanced relationships, family challenges, and often, legal complications.

These are all indications of low self-esteem and produce stressors that exacerbates (or intensifies) the core issues. This difficulty in managing stress is common with low self-esteem. The harder the person tries to perform well, the greater the difficulty. Longing for the approval of others, their activities become performance based; sometimes we call this people pleasing. Rather than doing what is the next right thing because it is the right thing, they are in a constant performance mode, seeking approval of others for their contribution.

As much as this is a self-perception problem, understand that no one gets into a state of low self-esteem alone, and no one gets out of low self-esteem without others. The causes are wide ranging.

Longing for the approval of others, their activities become performance based.

One of my personal challenges with low self-esteem came by way of the school I attended growing up. Like most schools, we had gym classes and other opportunities to play sports. I was not good at any of these activities. I had not learned at home or from family members. I had no older brothers to teach me and we lived miles out in the country on a farm. When it came to sports, I was the last one picked for the team.

I was teased and called names, as kids do to each other. It was a message that I was not able to contribute, so I was always on the outside looking in. If I had been taught how to play sports, I might have been able to do the physical things required. But the inability to do so fed the poor perception I had of myself.

When I joined the Marine Corps, this did change. Boot camp taught me I could do anything the others were doing. Not with gentle encouragement, but I got the lesson. By the time I finished Infantry Training, that dimension of low self-esteem was pretty much gone. Not to say that other parts of my life were not plagued by the often and awful feelings.

To gain your self-esteem you need to do esteem-able things. When people note your good job, you will naturally feel better about yourself. You didn't get it alone and you can't get out of it alone.

If the person battling with low self-esteem is left alone in their own self-evaluation, this personal ethos predictably transitions downward and manifests as low self-worth. Not necessarily the same phenomenon, but it has quite a similar core cause.

Self-esteem is that you don't feel you can do anything of importance; low self-worth is that you don't feel that as a person you are of any value.

Low Self Worth:

Low self-worth is how you see yourself and what you believe, you as a person, are worth. Believing you are not appreciated or held in any regard, importance or respect by others or even by yourself. The difference between low self-esteem and low self-worth is this: With the self-esteem issue, you made a mistake and with the self-worth issue your are the mistake.

I knew a man, many years ago, who was the most talented of musicians. His guitar playing was spoken of by the elite of the music world as genius. I personally would marvel and I must confess, as a guitar player even envied the skill, creativity and ease with which he played. He was a man of faith with strong conviction and knowledge and known in the community as a loving husband and a good father. All these things being said, he remained penniless, broke. Abject poverty seemed to be his lot in life.

His perception of money was distorted. Actually in his mind, his ability to make money was just not apparent. If he could have seen his abilities as others saw them, his musical gifting would have catapulted him into wealth. Minimally, he could have used the gift to produce a decent income.

But his perception was off. How he saw himself and how he perceived that others saw him, was the core challenge. His ability to measure his worth seemed to be non-existent. This whole issue is fostered by "what we think others think of us".

Early in my sobriety, I had tremendous concern that others were talking about me. If I came into a room and folks were sitting together laughing, I assumed that they were laughing at me or talking about me. So, challenging it, I brought the issue to my then sponsor.

He smiled and asked me why I thought I was so important that everyone was focused on me. It wasn't that they were talking about me, or didn't like me, the fact was that they likely didn't even know me or take notice of me.

I worked on this very troubling situation for some time, until I finally moved past it. One day I told my sponsor, "When I come into the room, I no longer feel that they are talking about me". In typical sponsor fashion, he said, "Just because you don't feel like they are, doesn't mean they're not".

People still talk about others and I suppose even about me. The difference is that I'm no longer basing who I am solely by what others say. Do I care what they think? Yes, but I am not basing who I am on it.

There is a cultural inaccuracy in the recovery circles. "What others think of you is none of your business". This is a band-aid type statement, designed to get people to stop obsessing on what others think. If taken literally, it creates a true attitude of indifference.

Do I care what others think of me? Well, of course. I want my children and grandchildren to respect me. My employers to value me and for folks at church to think well of my participation. Do I stay up nights worrying about what they think? No, I don't. I know myself well enough that I am confident that others will, for the most part, think and speak well of me.

It follows that if I don't care what others think, it is likely that I will get tangled up in self-depreciating words. Sometimes I will find myself saying the opposite of what I think or mean, just to appease others. Being either overly concerned or not concerned at all of others opinion of me, is a byproduct of low self-worth.

To break this dreadful cycle, I had to invest in myself. I started studying and went back to get a formal education. I began to read daily and take care of my physical condition. Not because I have something to prove, but more that I have chosen to place a high value on me.

When we live with low self-worth long enough, it takes us to the next aspect of how we see ourself, known as no self-image. If we live in a state of feeling poorly about ourselves long enough, we lose our identity. We will not be able to find our purpose in life or what God called us to be.

No Self Image:

No self-image or even a diminished self-image is an indicator that a person is unsure of who they are or what they believe or what they are to do. No self-image a byproduct of low self-esteem and low self-worth.

If they were completely honest, it would be discovered that they drift in and out of knowing themselves. We grow as individuals and pass through various stages of our lives and morph from one identity to another.

I have been through a season of life where I was the young invincible man, able to be and do anything and everything. I suppose the time I spent in the Marines had a large effect on my self-image for that season. There were no concerns for the tomorrows and little for other people. I simply charged forward taking on all comers.

I eventually became the dad and much of my self-image was caught up in this new role. I spent every day consumed with my children, their food, their clothes, their schooling, their health and their happiness. I was a dad and everything I did revolved around that important and blessed role.

I served as a pastor and in that season, I was identified as such by others. I look back and that seemed to be more others labeling me than my perception of myself. I recall the first time someone referred to me as Pastor David. It was foreign and felt odd. Over many years, I carried that title and served several congregations. Today I am occasionally referred to with that title from people who have known me for a lot of years. It makes me smile to hear it.

I have been a worker among workers and the executive management leader. The student during one season and the teacher in another. Now I'm the steady reliable husband, a grandpa and, of course, a writer.

All of the roles and titles we have had in life make up in part "the who" we are. The between each of these life seasons is a space and time, sometimes short, other times longer, but measurable. During these off times when we are not identified by a job or relationship, during the gap times, the in between times, who am I?

It would seem that in the world of addiction, the idea of newly sober people not knowing who they are is a common challenge. It really isn't that they don't know who they are, but more that they are no longer sure of what they believe, what they think, or how they should act or react to life.

We see this in troubled marriages that are struggling just to continue. One person or the other will express that they just don't know who they are. Sometimes people simply walk away; they leave, trying to find themselves. This often appears in teens and during seasons when a person is going through a transition. There is a lost identity; a state of no self-image.

No self-image is a byproduct of low self-esteem and low self-worth.

Often evident in co-dependency, as they have been trying to survive living in a relationship with the addict, they begin to suffer from no self-image. It is not exclusive to co-defendants, but is sometimes easier to identify.

Those in active addiction often experience this phenomenon. Chasing from one thing to another; one job to another, one relationship to another, even one religion to another. Never quite sure who they are, they attach themselves to relationships, possessions, and even geographical places, trying to find where they fit.

In this dimension of addiction, the addict is trying to become what they think everybody else wants them to be. They draw who they are by identifying themself with and by bonding to an external; as a sports spectator, a belief such as politics or religion, or engaging in a hobby. Often this self-identification is based on opinions or people they don't even know. Taking a stand on an issue and even joining a public protest; many are simply trying to find where they fit.

There is often a chameleon like persona. Attempting to distinguish themselves they work to create an image by imitating that which is around them. Their hope is that they can deflect others from seeing who they actually are or perhaps, who they are not. Some do find their footing and begin to build a foundation of self-choosing, forming a direction in life and committing to it. While others only shape a mirage of self, with spurious images that only last for short intervals.

Low self-worth, no self-image, and even low self-esteem are all rooted in the same seedbed of destruction called shame. Shame-based issues can stem from childhood trauma, the memory of life failures, or the repetitive sound of the words that were spoken aggressively against us.

I will discuss shame-based issues in the next segment at length. However, as a final thought on no self-image, I would add this. Any person who is being overshadowed by shame, will likely not become a whole person.

Shame Based Issues:

This takes us to last layer of our discursion; is what I call shame-based issues. This is actually the starting point for most addiction. The bedrock of all the emotional upheaval in addictions is shame. From it stem active addictions, destructive self-perceptions, inappropriate behaviors, flawed beliefs, and the shaping of invalid values.

Shame-based emotions are the feelings we get from something dishonorable, improper, or even ridiculous. It could be from something you have done or was done by someone else which negatively impacted you.

Growing up on a farm, we had our main meal in the late evening. We called it supper time. There was always more than enough to eat. In fact many times more food than was appropriate was out on my plate. We would have to eat everything on the plate, even if it was too much. "Clean off you plate, there are starving children all over the world." You were made to feel ashamed and guilty if you didn't eat everything.

Shame-based perspective is ultimately about feeling the need to hide from the people in your life and from the place where you live. Feeling humiliated or disgraced by things someone has done to you, or something that you have done, which you now regret. Shame becomes the lens that you see the world through. A feeling that one could like me, or want to be around me, because I'm broken or dirty.

Shame-based memories come from what has been done to you or by you that you don't want anyone else to find out. Some of it comes from those who have abused or taken advantage of you. You have a terrified view of the world as being not safe.

This is a devaluation of your opinions and thoughts of self. How you view yourself and what value you hold of who you are. Shame causes you to see yourself as inferior to others and to what you should be.

Your perception is that other people don't like you or won't except who you are because of this previous action. This corresponds to the low self-worth, low self-esteem, no self-image discussed. Trauma can cause a violation of your own values, opinions, and beliefs. It leaves you feeling completely disregarded and neglected.

Shame becomes the lens that you see the world though.

However, the memories remain and will produce internal self-degradation. These feelings often stay with you for a lifetime and will produce a tormented memory base. At this point, you are left with the view of being of little value. Shame is what you experience when you are disgraced, disrespected and your boundaries are violated. More than a feeling, it becomes a belief.

Guilt is a normal human emotion that is experienced when you do the wrong thing violating another's rights or failing to allow them a choice. An example would be a person who steals. The victim had no choice. You did wrong and you feel guilt.

Guilt is the normal human emotional response that comes from doing the wrong thing. Guilt is a message that tells you that you are violating your values; while shame is embracing the idea that what you value does not matter and is irrelevant.

If guilt is realizing that you have done the wrong thing, or erred either intentionally or unconsciously, then shame is believing that you are the wrong thing! It is embracing the idea that your mistake is who you are. Guilt makes the behavior stand out as contrary to who you believe you are. Shame causes you to believe that the behavior is who you are.

Shame is deeply tied to self-esteem because the more shame you carry, the less worthy you feel regarding yourself, and the less important your plans or actions seem. It is intrinsically linked to feeling flawed.

The guilt (normal) response to making a mistake is to admit you made a mistake, correct the behavior, and feel good about yourself because you have learned from it. The shame (abnormal) response to making a mistake is to try to hide your mistake. Believing that if others found out, they would think you are a terrible person. One is connected to a normal learning process, the other to a need to be seen as perfect. Feeling that mistakes make you a bad person.

Shame is readily linked to the feelings of inferiority described in the low self-image, low self-worth. When a person feels ashamed about himself it is linked to feeling inferior. After all, if shame makes the person feel that something is deficient, faulty, or lacking about himself, then he will compare himself to others. Comparing how he feels to how others look, he will automatically feel less capable of doing or being.

Comparing how you feel on the inside, to how others look on the outside.

The truth is that many people have been exposed to others who have made them feel ashamed of themselves. Often, these encounters have their roots in childhood. School, sports, and social settings often create a culture where shaming others is normal. I once heard a person use the term "shame factory" Those are places in life where we have learned to be ashamed of our behaviors, feelings, or failings.

Being corrected or told we were wrong in front of others, is particularly difficult for children, but has a similar impact on adults. There is a large difference in correcting a behavior and belittling the person. Those in authority, parents, teachers, or employers have this potential. Those who are not aware of the impact of their words, will unknowingly create shame, sometimes intentionally.

Many addicts were raised by extremely critical parents who made them feel ashamed about themselves. Being criticized or punished when we make mistakes, will produce shame. A parent may say, "You should be ashamed of yourself." If they only knew how much you already felt that way.

The Shame Dilemma:

1. Shame-based words produce feelings of being defective, damaged, fragmented or flawed.
2. Shame-based secrets create a sense of being dirty, unworthy, not pure.
3. Shame-based thinking causes images of being incompetent, worthless, invisible, unnoticed.
4. Shame-based relationships leave a sense that we are unlovable, not appreciated, not wanted, just wrong.
5. Shame-based emotions foster an awareness of insignificance, unimportance, failure.
6. Shame-based seasons limit potential. Thoughts during this period are on avoiding failure rather than making progress.
7. Shame-based settings are fearful, morbid, evil, dreaded.

8. Shame-based criticism cancels the effect of positive words and input.

Finding freedom from shame issues is both simple and difficult, at the same time. Simple to understand, difficult to actually do. Here are some things that you can do to overcome these painful memories.

Freedom from Memories:

- Own the memories. Write them down. Use enough detail to actually feel the feelings.
- Pray for the people who were involved in each of your episodes.
- Share the pain with a trusted person. Your 5th Step may be the appropriate setting or a spiritual advisor or therapist may be more appropriate. Each person is different.
- Protect yourself from thoughts that focus on a sense of victimization.
- Forgive the person or persons involved.
- Remind yourself that it is history, not your present reality.
- Ask God to remove the painful memories and to heal your mind and heart.
- Avoid repeated shame episodes. Establish good boundaries.

INVENTORY MAPPING

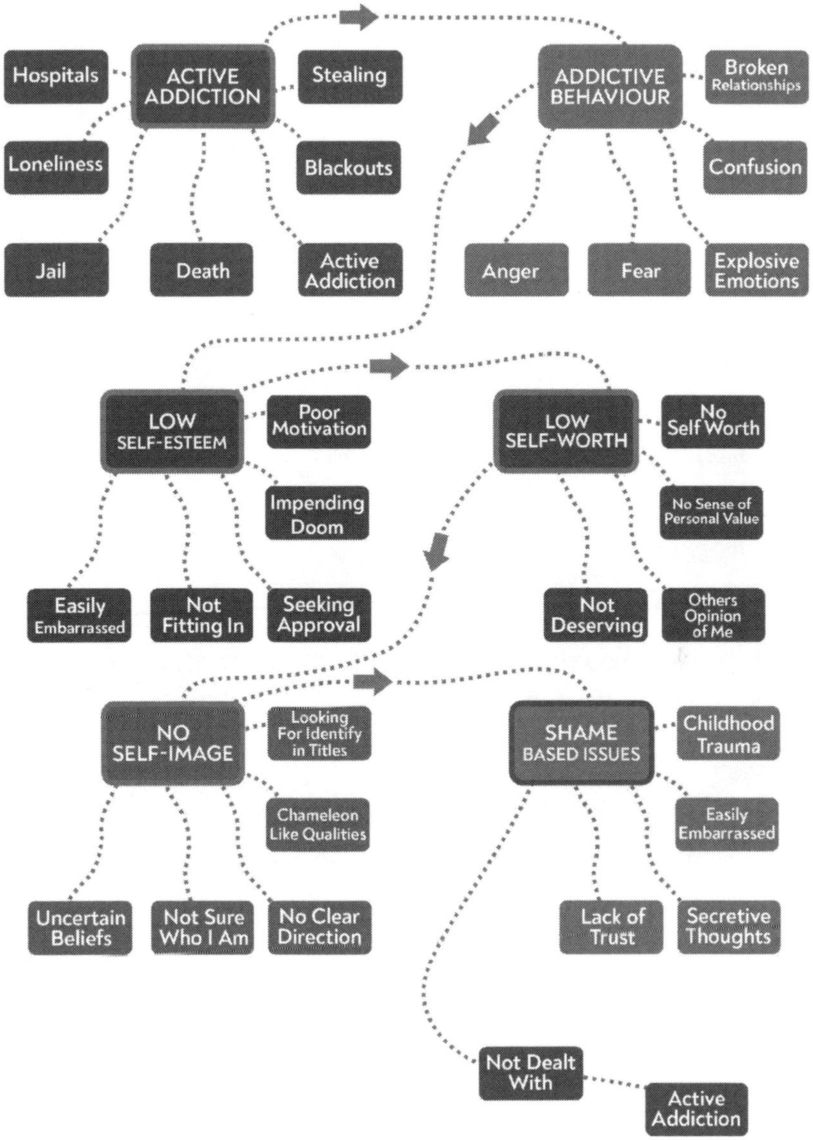

HERE IS A JOKE ABOUT TATER PEOPLE.

You have heard about Mr. Potato-head. Those who sit and watch TV all the time are known as Couch potatoes.

Here are some other taters you might know:

People who are content to watch while others participate are called -

Spec-taters.

People who never get around to actually getting up and doing something are referred to as –

Hesa-taters.

People who are phony and pretend to be someone they are not are referred to as –

Imma-taters.

People who are extremely bossy and are always telling others what to do are known as-

Dick-taters.

People who spend their time talking about the way others do things are labeled as –

Comen-taters.

People who stir up trouble and cause problems by getting others to complain are called —

Agie-taters.

People who are always friendly and will do what they say they will and are always ready to help are, of course –

Sweet-taters.

CHAPTER 7

CAPACITY, DISCIPLINE, AUTHENTICITY

Measuring our Spiritual Condition

MUCH HAS BEEN SAID ABOUT the matter of being spiritually fit and about our spiritual condition. Many believe that all of sobriety hinges on this one thing. I'm inclined to believe this as well. For those coming out of a lifestyle of addiction and addictive behaviors, power is needed in our lives.

This chapter is devoted to a self-review of your spiritual condition and how to get the power to stay sober and ultimately change.

The Capacity to Receive Recovery

This lack of power is evident for those who have found themselves in the pathway of addiction. Locating power seems to be the likely place to started exiting out of addiction. There cannot be any option to get out of or to move on from the addictive behaviors with any permanence without access to some kind of power. For some, the idea is that they will use their willpower to change this life pattern. I was told that I could test my willpower the next time I had intestinal flu and see how well willpower works in controlling it. So what about will power to escape addiction, can it ever produce results?

In spite of all that has been said to the contrary, some do recapture their will power, exercise their will power and somehow seem to distance themselves and even leave the addiction behind. Is this common? No. Is it predictable? Again no. Is it permanent? Not likely. The lack of power over any life controlling addiction has at its core self-centered behavior. This is, in essence, the root problem.

Whatever the addiction may be, a persons free will was used at the entry point. The person was so desirous to change how they felt that they made the choice to begin using whatever they could find at the moment to adjust their feelings. This was a free will choice and it worked. The lift that was found in lighting of that first cigarette, the rush of the first winning jackpot, the escape from overindulgence of their favorite comfort food and, of course, the life disconnect that comes from the alcohol or drugs.

All were a matter of a free will choice. Well, at least they started that way.

So, was the person powerless from the first moment they stepped into what would become their addiction? Not for most. There is a wide range of levels depending on the type of indulgence, the personal physiological composition, the level of use and internal need to escape. For most, it is a gradual slipping away. A subtle release from personal choice to an increased need to find the relief.

I would note that many of those who become addicted to one thing may not find relief in a different choice. I found great relief in drinking and using, smoking and other things but found the gambling table left me flat from the beginning. Addiction is clearly not "one size fits all" and the logical conclusion must be that neither is recovery from addiction.

Addiction is clearly not one size fits all and the logical conclusion must be that neither is recovery.

We begin with some dimension of control and power. However,

the longer the usage continues the more power we give up. There is not an automatic instant powerlessness; it is a "by degrees" surrender. Progressively we find the release that comes from the behavior is more costly. There is a turning point where our usage becomes habit and habit becomes necessity. As free will has been surrendered in the addiction, the option of picking our choice back up is narrow at best.

It was a selfish act and a self-centered choosing. So, if self-will that has gone out of control is the problem, then self-will won't likely be the solution. In the surrender of our free will our power is lost. For most, the powerlessness experienced is so vast that it blocks even the rational thoughts offered by those trying to help.

Not just powerless over the substance but the loss extends to the person's thinking. Layers of denial drain the very energy and power necessary to effectively move back into a positive choice and not continue in the escape.

At the point that is commonly referred to as "hitting bottom", there comes a clarity that one has lost their choice in the matter. The seemingly harmless escape, that was so fulfilling at the start, is now the trap that has taken from them the power of choice and most everything in life that comes by way of good choices. Try as you may, the exercise of just willing it away or the old "just say no" seems to be of little help. For the person imbedded in the depths of addiction, will power does little good.

The capacity to find freedom or any facsimile of recovery on our own seems nonexistent. Like the dead battery in the car, it has lost it's power including the power to restart. If it could just get started, it's power would be restored, but no power is no power. Clearly the lack of power extends to not having enough power to even re-ceive power. In this state, the person holds zero capacity to receive power or recovery. Will power has failed to produce and something greater than the person, and their choice must be accessed.

As is often the case, another person will need to intervene and begin to exercise choice for the person caught in the trap. Much has been tried by way of intervention and it is sometimes the jump start that is needed to regain some control. The frustrated family member, boss or judge can, on occasion, impose some level of control. This is not a guarantee. There is no promise that personal control will be achieved. Is it worth a try? Of course.

The lifeline that allows a beginning point should be thrown out whenever and wherever it can. The recapture of a person's choices is rarely a one step process. No one arrives at addiction in one step and the reverse is also true. The capacity and option to find recovery, even if it is in a very embryonic state, should be grasped immediately.

Multiple Attempts

So to the onlooker, the person who continues to pick up their drug of choice, the drink or the addiction pacifier in whatever form it comes, seems to lack will or choice. It is neither. Not until the person finds some capacity to receive sobriety can any progress be realized. What opens a heart to allow the normality of sober thinking to begin to have influence? This hitting bottom is the place where someone comes out of desperation. They are essentially out of options physically, mentally, financially and spiritually. The capacity to accept recovery and sobriety is high at this point of desperation. This is usually where the collection of negative circumstances are too large to ignore.

The question is, does a person need to destroy their entire life before they can get to a place where the capacity to receive recovery exists? The answer is no. Many find some way to stop the madness before they meet total destruction.

The capacity to receive help arrives in a moment of clarity that comes to every person in addictive behavior. At some place and time, there is posed an internal question, "What am I doing?" There is a point that this internal question becomes, "I need to change. I need to stop."

This does not come only in the throes of disaster? People come to clarity at moments that you would not expect. Sometimes by observing someone who is suffering the byproduct of their own addiction. It could be a line in a movie. A moment in a church ceremony, like a wedding or a funeral. It varies from person to person, but it will always come.

You will have to admit defeat from your heart, and obviously no one can do that for you.

If the person is questioning themselves about their behavior and should vocalize it, they should be told to stop immediately. A challenge as simple as, "If you really are not addicted, it will be easy to stop, or if you are, it may be difficult." Those without an addiction leave the whole thing behind when the initial signs of trouble appear. It does not need to accelerate to total destruction for them to say enough already!

The necessity of multiple attempts to stop is commonplace. This is normal to the addicted and the clearest of signs that addiction is present. Some will say, never tell someone that they are an alcoholic or habitual gambler or even hooked on food. Let them find out for their selves. They have to admit it from their heart.

Yes, this is true; however, just ignoring the obvious and not saying anything is paramount to agreeing with them in their deception. The challenge may not work but needs to be presented anyway. They should know, without any doubt, what your position is regarding their behavior. If you reflect on it for a moment, the pathway for most coming out of addiction does not begin with ending the active addictive behavior, but with the challenge and a moment of clarity. It is as much a part of the journey as is celebrating the first year clean or finding God or any other part of the process.

Not many achieve success on the first try. However, it seems that with each approach, the capacity for success expands a little. Another excuse is shattered. Irrational thinking is exposed for what it is. Small successes should be celebrated. There is no accurate prediction of what level will the person expand their individual capacity enough to begin permanent recovery. But the capacity does expand with each attempt.

If you can follow the natural logic of lost control, then recapturing control becomes more tangible. We are not relegated to remain powerless forever. Can this be accomplished with a person's willpower? No, not likely; however, the exercise of choice becomes an intricate component.

Faith is an essential part of building capacity.

There will need to be something one can attach their free will to that contains more power than the addiction. Faith is an essential part of building capacity. Faith in something big enough to always work and connected enough for the individual to hold on to it. This is not really a mystery. It is common among all men and all societies, all races and cultures. The idea that power is available is universal. The power source is God. Great enough to control the universe, sufficiently personal to enter my free will space.

Clearly, the outright rejection of God was, at least in part, the cause of my lack of power to begin with. When I lack the capacity to receive power or recovery for that matter, I have one place to look. It was my free will all the time. Choosing alternative options to find comfort in a life that was anything but comfortable.

Leaving God behind, or never having a belief to start with. Depending on one's experience. Self-demands, self-centered behavior, and self-will out of control. Trying to find a way to relieve the pain and discomfort in everything. There it was all the time. God was the source of all power and the moment I connect with God, I am no longer powerless.

This is the beginning place of having the capacity to receive recovery. It starts with a connection with God to break the cycle of addiction. But it is convoluted thinking to believe that God is powerful enough to intervene in the cravings and lack of control regarding addiction, but that is as far as we can or should go with it.

He is big enough to remove the desire for alcohol or drugs, but not capable or willing to remove other flawed parts of my damaged character? Believing that he could bring a reprieve for a day so that my choice would be not to pick up, but relegating and limiting his involvement to just one area. A persons capacity to receive is only limited to their choice to believe. Faith should not end with entry levels of sobriety. That is the beginning point to limitless things that God will do, if we give him permission.

This is where capacity is of the essence. Should we move from calling on God for his help and then under a feigned humility stop the interaction? No, but many do this very thing.

Capacity grows with exposure, usage, and awareness.

One's capacity to grow in sobriety and recovery is limitless. Unless of course, you place your own limits on it. This capacity includes embracing freedom from cravings, removal of all destructive behaviors, repairing damaged relationships and building new relationships, finding health physically, mentally, emotionally, and spiritually.

The concept of limited recovery comes into play when we disregard our total void of any power in our lives. We then begin to believe that we can again enter into free will choices, that are based on a faulty internal belief system. We are only limited if we choose to limit God.

Our capacity to receive recovery grows with exposure, usage, and awareness. Attendance at meetings, working with the process of recovery, a sponsor, following the steps and reading, all expose us to the reality of our life. This applies to both the good and the bad.

The more we use the tools of getting clean and sober, the better we become. Similar to practicing a sport, music or work, the better we get. If we keep the matter of usage in place, we will improve always. The saying goes, "use it or lose it".

The more we are exposed to recovery, the more we will use it. The more we use it, the greater our awareness of how much progress we have made and how far we have yet to go.

The Discipline to Retain Recovery

Life disciplines are unique to each person. Depending on your personality, upbringing, environment and even your station in life. Disciplines are not one size fits all; however, they do fall within some natural parameters for everyone.

Some are naturally inclined toward a specific activity. Some have higher energy levels than others. Physical capabilities and mental attitude affect every part of our lives. These disciplines will always improve our chances of achieving the things we want to accomplish.

Included in the process of disciplines, of course, are physical, mental emotional and spiritual aspects. So let's touch on a couple of aspects, starting with the physical dimension.

The discipline to retain sobriety is connected to our health. Daily activities, like work, exercise and even diet are part of the process of keeping sober. Each of these impacts the way that we feel physically.

Attendance at recovery meetings, while at times may be enjoyable, the discipline to attend when you don't feel like it, or don't have enough time is essential.

There is the practice of routinely connecting to others in sobriety. Some times in person, other time on the phone. The method is not as important as the cultivation of relationships. We have discovered that staying clean and sober alone is the most difficult way to approach this challenge. Forming the practice of saying out of isolation is clearly an exercise of wisdom.

Of all the areas that we need the forms of discipline, the spiritual life is the most important. We are given a repose from living and dying in active addiction based on developing our spiritual life. There are specific practices that foster success in this dimension of sober life.

Disciplines include prayer, purity of focus and obedience.

Prayer and its relationship to recovery is an imperative for maintaining long term recovery. Prayer is not a quick fix for a life not lived right. It is more of a byproduct and a reward for those who live with integrity. Make right choices and your prayer life will come alive. Make poor choices and the prayer will be a chore, filled with distractions.

Time in the presence of God is the reward of a life lived with the discipline of prayer. As many believe that heaven is the ultimate reward in the life to come, a conscious connection with God's presence is a bit of heaven in advance.

Not until a man has walked day to day with the presence of God, will he be able to really believe. Overcoming doubts about the existence of God is not found in theological debate. Belief in God is not found by witnessing people in worship on Sunday morning or at the Saturday evening recovery meetings. The evidence of God never comes by explanation but by revelation.

It is not necessarily in the big miracles that true faith is established. It is more often found in the walking out of day-to-day activities that God is revealed. It is in the asking of small things with frequency, where you will see God answer and allow you to experience His presence.

God's true nature of immense love and always caring attentiveness. This will be revealed as you move through your routine activities each day. Knowing God is with you like a companion, a friend and always willing to be your help. Not just in the difficulties but in the simplistic, most times, routine activities, God will show up.

God's true nature is immense love.

If you walk with God in the discipline of prayer, while living in this life, when you finish this life and enter the eternal, you will be right at home. If you have not practiced the presence of God or the daily walking out of that connectivity when you pass from this life, you will find yourself a little out of place.

If you do not know what to pray, what to say, or what the protocol is to approach God, I'm pretty sure you will make something up. Prayer becomes random, unproductive and sort of an add-on to life. This is the core reason that people have such a difficult time with their faith.

Compare making a connection to God, to our routine of connecting with people. We start by gettin to know a little about them. It doesn't always take a lot to start, so we start with their name. The most important word in the human language, any language, is your name.

When you hear your name, it immediately validates you as a person. It separates you from everyone else in the moment. Your sense of worth, belonging, and connectivity are all established when your name is spoken.

In my years of management, even with larger groups of employees, I set my mind to learn people's names. As much as possible I made it a point to connect with each employee everyday.

My discipline was to walk through each department and call each person by name. I would give them a hug as well. This discipline drew us together in a relationship beyond the normal employer/employee connection. It made all the difference in how we worked together. Many have become lifelong friends and we are connected to this day. Even the ones I had to terminate are still my friends. Why? Because I took the time to learn about them, starting with their name.

So how much more is God's name of value? Since we are trying to make this spiritual connectivity and our goal is to establish a communication with God, it would seem vital that we first know Gods name. I have learned so much about God by the way he reveals himself to us in his many names.

This is where the conflict arises; many people pray to the unknown God. How can you build intimacy, communication or even connection without first knowing his name? It is foundational; however, people often resist even the idea.

Most often I hear people say things like, "I'm not religious, I'm spiritual". The Bible gives us a reflection of those who were considered religious. These were the people who prayed to the unknown God. The apostle Paul said to them, "I see you're quite religious".

Of course, if I told you that you were religious because you pray to the unknown God, you might be offended. Oh well it wouldn't be the first time.

It becomes easier to pray to God when we see his character and love for us.

Spirituality is experiencing some form of connection to God or link to some power greater than yourself. What ever that may be. For one person being in nature seems to make the connection. For another a drum circle brings the feeling. Meditation for another does it.

Religion is taking a spiritual experience and using it routinely to make the feeling connection over and over. Most recovery meetings start with the Serenity Prayer. Why because it produces a spiritual feeling and sense of connection to God. We do it over and over that is religion. This is of course connecting to the unknown God. It is limited and will produce very little in the way of spiritual growth. Some after many years of such practice are no further along the when they began. Why? Because they only know about God, they don't really know God. Religion will always keep you trapped at an entry level.

The religion that we want to separate ourselves from is spawned from our uncertainty of who God is. Religion is actually interpreted as "a return to bondage". "Bondage to what?", you ask. Fear. There are innumerable kinds of fear and, connecting to the unknown God is just one of those.

Then, let me give you a glimpse into the many names of God. Buddhists call him Buddha; Muslims call him Allah. The Jewish people will not even write the name of God because it seemed to be too holy. Everyone has a concept they use to approach God.

I knew a man who believed God›s name was Emmett. The entire

scope of his theology was based on the fact that he had never met a man named Emmett that he didn't like. So I asked him the hard questions. "Is Emmett always around? Does Emmett really love you? Was Emmett able to rescue you from your addiction? Could Emmett give you the grace to build relationships with other people?" The answer to each question was ,"I don't know". Clearly Emmett was an unknown God.

The Bible has over 100 names to describe God. We get to know God's character by understanding His names. One of the many reasons I choose to believe and connect with God, as he is described in the Bible, is because of the many names that describe who he is. I didn't really find that description anywhere else. It becomes easier to pray to God when we see his character and love for us.

Part of the discipline to receive recovery is to be grounded spiritually. The moment you choose to open yourself up to a greater understanding of who God is, will be the moment your spiritual life opens up. Prayer becomes effective and fluid.

Authenticity to Transmit Recovery

Authenticity includes willingness, opportunity, and perception. Be open, be available and be transparent.

Personal authenticity in its simplest form, is simply being who you represent yourself to be; not one of those people trying to portray themselves as someone they are not. Without being authentic, you will come across as disingenuous and plastic. It seems that such people only portray part of their life and that as something that it's not.

The challenge with being authentic comes from people's perception of you. If you are seen as a phony in one area of your life, you will come across as a person who cannot be trusted at all. Should your reputation become that of a duplicitous character, you will be ever limited in connecting with others. Not just the connection with people who may lend assistance to your recovery, but those that you may encounter that need your help.

Authentic people are known as being the most trustworthy. Their reputation precedes them, and they have a good name. These are the folks who are positioned to provide genuine help for those seeking recovery.

To present yourself as a recovery person who is authentic, there are a few things you need to remember.

1. **Be yourself.** There is only one of you so be that person. Trying to emulate someone that you admire will cause the real you to disappear. We need the real you. Your experience, perspective and words are one of a kind.
2. **Do what you say you will do.** If you give out your phone number, be available to answer. If you agree to meet up, show up and be on time. Don't make a plan and then make an excuse. Made up excuses are always easy to see through.
3. **Participate in recovery with the newcomer.** Do this both at meetings and one on one. How will the person you are helping understand the importance of connection and participation at meetings, if you don't demonstrate it? Just talking about it carries little impact.
4. **Avoid financial transactions.** Lending money or borrowing money from those you are positioned to help will cloud the relationship. I have seen money wreck many good friendships and families. Nothing will strip you of being authentic any faster than misunderstandings over finances.

5. **Same gender relationships.** In the process of helping others historically same gender connections seem to have better success. Men with men and women with women. The cross-gender sponsorship will create unnecessary challenges.

   If the person you are trying to help has a spouse, girlfriend or boyfriend, the time you spend one on one might be suspect. Even if your motives are right, it sends the wrong message. The same suspicion may come from your relationship. Your motives may be upright, but we open the door for those who are predatory.

6. **Avoid Recovery Romance.** Stay away from romantic relationships in the recovery circles. They are allowed but most often will cloud other people's perception of who you are and what your real motives are. Your efforts will most often be clouded by this.

7. **Carry yourself with gratitude.** Show it in your words, reactions to others and willingness to serve without recognition. Years on the podium and on the stage have taught me that someone is always watching. Someone is always listening.

8. **Don't rely on profanity.** Speak from your own experience and avoid barroom and street talk. When a person is expressing themselves using excessive, frequent, and aggressive profanity, it is seen as a sign of spiritual immaturity and deficiency. It serves no useful purpose and is, in fact, a mask for and a demonstration of insecurity and low self-esteem. It is a learned behavior that, in the mind of the user, becomes a social lubricant. To others a sign a clandestine person.

9. **Be the solution.** The primary key to authenticity is to be the solution. Be filled with compassion for others. The day you lose your need for personal recovery, you also lose your influence to help other people. It may not be instantaneously, but it is eventually the downfall of your ability to help people. Inadvertently you will begin to speak down to people as opposed to speaking into their hearts from a place of equality.

Compassion never flows downhill, it only will work on a horizontal plane.

This old couple were getting more and more forgetful so they went to the doctor to see if there was anything that they could do. The doctor encouraged them to start writing things down. He said that writing notes to themselves would help them remember short term and improve their memory in the long run.

That night, after dinner, the husband suggested,

“Let’s have some ice cream.” His wife said, “Sounds good.”

“What flavor would you like?” he asked.

“I’ll have chocolate. But you better write that down, so you don’t forget”

“Come on” he said. “I can remember one thing. Chocolate ice cream. Do you want Cool Whip on it?"

“Yes, I would like that. But write that down so you don’t forget.”

“Nonsense! I can remember two things without writing them down. Chocolate ice cream and Cool Whip. Do you want sprinkles on it?"

“You know I like sprinkles on my ice cream. But you better write it down”.

“Oh for crying out loud! I’m not senile. I can remember three things. Chocolate ice cream, Cool Whip and sprinkles.»

A few minutes later he returned from the kitchen with a plate of bacon and eggs. His wife looked at him and said:

“I told you to write it down, you stubborn old man. You forgot the toast!”

CHAPTER 8

THREE ENEMIES OF RECOVERY

Ignorance, Forgetfulness and Laziness

There are fundamentally three basic enemies of addiction recovery. I'm sure you could identify wrong thinking, cravings, triggers and other matters, but after 40 years of staying sober, I would submit that they mostly fall into one of these categories.

In this chapter we will explore each of these ideas and learn how they war against our sobriety and recovery. While reading this chapter, be aware of the mental pictures you have of your life in recovery. Each time you have a mental picture, pause to see how the discourse actually affects you and impacts your life.

Ignorance

We will start with ignorance. The other observations and experiential understandings will be developed out of this first premise. As we enter into addiction recovery, we are basically ignorant of our demise. We may have some common knowledge about addiction from a cultural understanding, but at the beginning we have little real insight about the nature of addiction or grasp its true impact on our lives. If we are looking for the core issue of our addiction, we should test them for ignorance and self-centeredness before we test them for drugs.

We tend to believe and listen to what we already know. We are drawn to those things that are familiar and support what represents our worldview. Each person will be inclined to attend to the data that best supports their life view. Wallowing in addiction, we formulated a picture of a life revolving around our using.

Often to the point that we remained ignorant of the most important things. The result was that we failed to learn many of the basics of living. So ignorance became an unknown enemy and a subtle foe. Slick, confusing and so deceptive. We thought we knew everything; we had all the answers. Sadly, we had answers to nothing that really mattered. For the most part it wasn't about us having the answers, we didn't even know the questions. Now we discover that it is time to get cleaned up and grow up.

Our initial entry into recovery and the obvious starting point for a new life is then based on learning. Learning about addiction, how to get free from it and how to change your life once you become liberated from active addiction. What each of us will bring to the table is a bank of information that we have learned in our lifetime. Our lifetime of addictive behaviors fostered by hurt, disappointment, fear and anger.

Some of what we have learned is true and accurate. Other parts are the repugnant byproduct of our wrong thinking, misinformation and even some outright falsehoods that we embraced as truth. Immersed in a survival mode of living, our defenses are up and our minds are closed to new ideas. We are terrified of change and resistant to anyone telling us what to do.

- - - know the answers, we didn't even know the questions.

By whatever method our pathway got us to recovery, we are here.

Those who have arrived before us reach out and tell us what they feel will help. Immediately we begin to compare what we know or think we know, to what is being presented. Making our comparison, we evaluate and process all that we hear, based on what we know or believe we know.

So often the wrong mindset distorts what is being given to us for our benefit and our learning. We mentally review what we know, our own bank of misinformation, believe it is accurate and cling to it like a life preserver. This happens in part, because of the familiarity and comfortability of our own thoughts. Because we have nothing we trust, we allow little in to unseat and replace faulty thinking.

We can only draw from the information that we have. In order to evaluate what is coming our direction, we have to trust the information. Contrary to the very things we have been taught, trust no one, be skeptical of everything and never allow anyone to get too close. We have to take the risk. Trust is a risk successfully survived. So it becomes a clear imperative that we must, on some level, trust the people that are trying to teach us, accept their version of truth and the basis of such truth.

And often in our haste to be right, we immediately want to correct and even rewrite the text we are studying to fit our version of what it should be. We fail to look at the positive effect it has had on others who have studied and applied it to their lives. This happens in business, religion, family relationships and even in the understanding of our own health. Not only do we resist the information designed to propagate change, but much of the time we take up an opposing position, desperately attempting to persuade and ultimately convince those who would teach us that they should learn from us.

This is particularly prominent in learning recovery. We come with paralyzing fears of being hurt again or hurting others. We come with anger over wrongs that have been done and perceptions of how others have treated us. We come with memories of failure that we have tried to superimpose on others as the cause for our limitations in life.

Saddled with the baggage of a life poorly lived, we don't trust others. Simply put, we can't understand their motives. Why would someone want to help me and what are they trying to get from me? This ignorance will keep us trapped in a basic distrust that will ultimately block life-giving thought and words. The very things that will produce relief and start recovery, we resist. The resistance in this case is true ignorance.

The word ignorance comes from the Latin word *ignōrantia.* It means *to completely ignore, avoid noticing and finally to reject due to lack of evidence.*

Ignorance is derived from the word ignore. Those newly in recovery from addiction are masters at turning a blind eye to what is blatantly obvious to others. It is ignoring both intentionally and perpetually.

People tend to ignore the things that are important. This is often seen in taking time with their marriage, quality activities with the kids, a positive church connection, and even focusing on those things that impact and develop good health.

The areas of life that we need to not be ignorant of are those that bring setbacks, trouble or destruction; these should be at the top of the pay attention list. We should not ignore those things that are the "Always Fails" failures in our lives. Particularly when these are overtly routine or successive failures.

At the very top of the list of things that we need to learn, is how to be honest about our particular set of circumstances. It is called "life on life's terms". How we process through circumstances, what our responses to others are and the effort that we are willing to put forth to become responsible and successful. Life on life's terms encompasses the entire mind set of giving up the right to blame circumstances, others and even God. Accepting the necessity for rules, work, restraint, and obligation.

Learning about addiction, its impact and its deception, would certainly be on the list of things to learn. However, simply learning about the principles of addiction and gaining some knowledge of recovery may not suffice.

Should we embrace all there is to know about our condition and fail to take on the obligation to actually change, we will be ignorant of the true purpose and opportunities of life. The spectrum includes learning what it takes to get free from addiction, what tools are available to overcome the addictive behavior, and how to remain diligent to the task.

Most of my spiritual awakenings have been preceded by a rude awakening.

On the subject of being ignorant, self-centeredness is a common blind spot. It is at the center of all our addict comportment. It would seem on most levels we were deficient in the basic competencies necessary to forge a healthy relationship with anyone. Friendship, business partnership or family kinship, our connectivity was resolutely lacking.

The know-how required to build bridges and relationships has evaded us. Most people in addiction have ignored their relationships long enough that there has been little left in the aftermath but destruction. Obviously, it will take direct and deliberate effort to regain some facsimile of normal. The reality of this life driven by self-centered thinking and behavior becomes the rude awakening.

Most of my spiritual awakenings have been preceded by a rude awakening.

Being taught skills to have a healthy relationship will need to follow a genuine awakening to the ugly truth. We have used and abused everyone who has entered our life. Some honest repentance, repose, rejuvenation and restoration will be necessary.

We need not be ignorant of what we do not know. We need to learn what we need to learn. At this point, we don't know what it is that we don't know. If we will be genuine, make the effort to connect, ask the questions and practice listening, the answers will come.

For the majority of us, we will suddenly learn what we don't know. It includes who we need to connect with, what we owe by way of restitution and how to rebuild after the devastation. Ignorance of how to have a relationship, a job, and a family is overtly compounded when we add alcohol, drugs or other addictions to the mix. The mix puts the self-centered life on steroids.

Forgetfulness

Forgetfulness is the second enemy of recovery that I will address.

So, let me ask you, "What have you forgotten lately?" Everybody forgets things from time to time, that's pretty natural but there are some things that would be best if they were forgotten. There are those things also that should be always be remembered. What we don't pay attention to, may all too quickly be forgotten.

Often what we learn is stored away somewhere, for another day and another time. We make a conscious effort to remember it, in the moment, but then later on it fades.

This is really common with conferences that ww attend. We garner loads of new information about subjects that, at least at the beginning, had a high interest to us. We listen to entertaining speakers, watch multiple media presentations and even sometimes take voracious notes. In our process of learning, we try to connect what we have learned. We seek memorable and interesting ways to apply it in our life, our business, or family.

It is the latest information on the most interesting of topics available when we receive it. Then we go back to real life. We get on the plane and fly home and we tell our spouse all about the wonderful things we learned. Sometimes we share with a coworker the tremendous book that we just read and how greatly it has impacted us.

May you be able to keep what is worth remembering, and misplace what is better off forgotten.

Then life happens. We watch movies, surf the Internet, connect with our friends on Facebook, go out to dinner and we even listen to the news (not recommended). Barraged with layers of new information; the latest greatest information that we find on our favorite subject. Then the one thing we meant to retain, suddenly fades. All too soon it just blends into everything else that we have learned. It no longer is the priority and so we no longer retain it as vital information.

I have looked back at notes from conferences and not only was I not impressed, I couldn't even imagine why I went to the conference to start with. But it happens because we change. We continue to grow; we continue the process and of course, we forget what we were sure would be with us forever.

Forgetting what we no longer need, might be a good thing in some ways. Singer / song writer, Paul Simon, wrote in one of his hits, "When I think back on all the crap I learned in high school, it's a wonder I can think at all." There are some things I just flat out forgot, for good reason. Other things that I simply "failed to remember". Then there are the memories worthy of my "essential retention". We are all like that. Even some of these are too soon forgotten.

The danger is in forgetting things that we desperately need to put into motion in our lives. Some pieces of information are so vital, that we need to purposefully choose to preserve them. So the second enemy of sobriety is that "forgetting space". We forget what we have learned, forget what we have agreed to believe and put into practice, forget the sober life and then eventually forget where we came from.

Our commitment to change, to believe in God, allowing healing to enter our life, and building a life with those we love, has somehow lost its priority. So, many return to their addiction. They unknowingly slip back into their old life. The idea that they just slipped up and failed is erroneous. No one accidentally, unknowingly just goes back. Look at a S.L.I.P. as "Sobriety Loses It Priority".

After so much difficulty, what causes us to suddenly forget? There are a variety of causations, however it is not normally a sudden occurrence. I see it as a slow fade. A gradual and continuous process. We stop doing the little daily things that made all the difference. We happily went to meetings, persistently spent prayer time, freely stopped to help others. Now it seems to all have changed, suddenly? No, the gradual eroding of the commitments comes with the encroachment of self-centered thinking and behavior.

If you fail to remember where you came from, you are likely to return there with very little forethought or resistance.

The only thing about it is that suddenly, "I'm back"! We have moved far enough in the direction of how we used to be that now we tip the scales. It wasn't one thing, but the accumulation of thoughts, attitudes and words. The old person that you were, the one that you bid adieu and thought you would never see again, has returned. How could this unspeakable thing happen, so suddenly? Let's explore.

Forgetfulness is derived from a variety of factors. For those in long term sobriety, the chief factor is boredom. Attendance at meetings where you see the same people and make good friendship style connections is, for the most part, positive. You can safely share your difficulties and get positive feedback, at least in theory.

The challenge comes in hearing the same old stories over and over. The well rehearsed, overused lines repeated over and over. "Don't drink and go to meetings, keep it simple, one day at a time and the ever present, my Higher Power, that I choose to call God". So we become bored with the whole process.

Staying sober becomes routine. While routine has its place, for those addicted boredom can set it. Call it what you like, restless, discontented, unmoved, but it is real. Where is the excitement? Where is the fun? The adrenaline that came with the old life is not being activated. It somehow seems we are suffering from "terminal serenity". So our interest fades. What was at one time an exciting proposition, our very delight, now has become somewhat of a tiresome duty on our best days and laborious drudgery on the worst. I would note that if you are bored, you are equally boring.

Perhaps it is time to change meetings, read some new books and intentionally move forward. Boredom comes from the stagnation of growth. Perhaps you have worn out this level of sobriety and spiritual life. You have found a plateau that has you trapped. You must make some changes and, quite simply and frankly, need to advance. Make the move from being the bleeding deacon to the elder statesman. If you fail to grow, you will have to go. Start speaking something fresh and alive instead of always repeating the same dead, lifeless, spiritually deficient words.

Tied intrinsically to the enemy of forgetting, is life's turmoil. At the top of the list is sickness. Everyone has times when sickness overtakes us. The common cold or the flu is sufficient to cause us to become less mindful. We procrastinate in doing the things that work and forget the importance of the small things. "As soon as I feel a little better", "I need to get some rest", "I'm just not up to it". Everyone has these times. I say rest, get well and don't infect others. But when you do get better, don't forget the little things that made all the difference in staying sober.

If you fail to grow, you will have to go.

Often the turmoil of life becomes the distractor. Sickness is only one of many. Getting dismissed from employment or other financial reversals. Being behind on monthly bills or having accumulated large debt over an extended period of time. So we get a second job and for some, even a third. Committed to eradicating the indebtedness, everything else takes on less emphasis and concern.

Legal complications from a divorce or a law suite can disrupt every area of your life. They can, in a short time, become all consuming. How soon we forget the daily practice of connecting to others, studying or prayer. Many important matters are neglected during the process. When the turmoil passes and we regain some facsimile of normal, without being mindful of the things we did to get clean and sober, and then to stay clean and sober, may well get lost in the shuffle.

We forget to help ourselves and of course, neglect totally our pledge and responsibility to reach out to others. Long-term sobriety is intrinsically linked to our willingness to help other people. Our commitment to bring assistance to those struggling in sobriety is somehow forgotten, along with the rationale that we embraced when we placed the oath in our hearts to do so.

What is it that you have forgotten? I have never met anyone who has returned to their addiction that has not, in some manner, forgotten. Where they came from, what they gained in recovery or their various commitments to themself, God, and others. We need to be reminded of all the times we've been told, "did you remember to" or "don't forget". Remembering becomes a conscious effort to prioritize our recovery; an effort that will one day save our lives.

Laziness

Once you have learned and exercised diligence to remember what is important, there's only really one other internal motivation that would take you back out and it is called laziness.

Let's discuss this matter of being lazy. There is a laziness that comes on purpose or with intention. Those that are see themselves as entitled and feel that it's not necessary to put in any effort to receive the reward. Others should work and give them money or they should be eligible to be promoted like anyone else, even though their effort is minimal.

Laziness is best described as the lack of willingness to put in a sufficient amount of effort to accomplish whatever the task might be. Often the energy and effort withheld is done so with intention. For some, this is a learned behavior

However, there is a laziness that comes as a matter of a slow fade and lack of attentiveness. Laziness is not always a product of poor motivation, but some laziness is acquired simply by inactivity.

Look at the matter of personal fitness. My real-life experience has been that the more I exercise and the more energy I put into physical activity, the more energy I will have. Then it follows that the better my motivation seems to be.

There is a parallel in the process of recovery from addiction. A lot of the failure in addictions recovery is do to laziness and the issue of having a poor attitude. Much of the diminished impetus fosters laziness. This laziness is a byproduct of the corresponding inactivity and the unwillingness to put in any level of quality effort.

The diminished effort and activity often are derived from a dysfunctional prioritization. Things don't seem to be as important as they were in the beginning. Somehow I'll stay sober just on the momentum that I've gained from my efforts in the past. We tend to bank on the reconnection of our past achievements. Many recovering alcoholics and addicts have fallen into the trap of allowing vigilance to fade. The reality of sobriety is that it requires vigilance. One of our older members, who has now passed used to say,

"Eternal vigilance is the price of permanent sobriety."
George Campus

Failure to maintain diligence over an addiction can cause the onset of forgetting that addiction is insidious, cunning, progressive, and fatal.

Addiction tends to somehow mask itself well. It, for a time, fades into the background and eventually it seems to become nonexistent. For those that are unaware, when least expected, this addiction will rear its ugly head. Often bewildered by the outcome, the person who thought they were totally free is suddenly in the quagmire again.

This is best explained by understanding that addiction is put into remission and we are never really cured. Observation has been that many upstanding men and women who found recovery, got lazy and stopped maintaining the readiness to respond to the day of temptation.

So the watchfulness becomes less evident. The necessity to attend recovery meetings, read books on recovery, stay connected to others in recovery, diminishes. It becomes increasingly difficult to mentally justify the expenditure of energy on something that seems to have been resolved.

Laziness feeds the common trait of procrastination. We put off what we could do today, what should be done, until tomorrow or some other time. Often, we will do just enough to appease our conscience, then we put off even thinking about it.

Procrastination is the lack of willingness to do today, what will tomorrow be even more difficult.

Procrastination will inevitably lead us to disappointment. Each time the idea of what we should be doing comes and is dismissed, it becomes less likely that we will believe that it was important. Those that engage in this process with regard to their recovery will become disappointed in the result. Apparently attending meetings and doing the steps doesn't work after all; I tried it and was no better off than when I started.

Then comes the element of unbelief. Unbelief is characteristically found in a person who believed but now does not. Belief is the prerequisite to unbelief. When we fail to continue to do what has produced success in the past, it normally follows that the measure of success shrinks with the diminished activity.

We then hope against hope that the success we attained will remain and the negative challenges will be gone forever. But it rarely works that way. We stop what brought about the prosperity and advancement and not only does the good disappear, but the old characteristics and failings return.

If the past is defining us, we will try to leave behind the things that produced the bad. The challenge is that we often leave the good behind as well. We must recapture the good and add something better to it, in order to leave the past behind.

Conclusion

In this present-day culture, these three enemies predominantly ride in on the waves of being overly busy, what is commonly called the tyranny of the urgent. There is the cacophony of sound, the noise that comes as a constant barrage stealing serenity, and the overwhelming number of people who crowd into our lives. These enemies work to keep us engaged in the deception of "more is better" and "sooner rather than later". Enough is never enough and hurry displaces patience.

Needing more is not a symptom of a problem; it is the problem.

So we choose to resist the adversarial attackers that war against our staying clean and sober. We only take up the things that are essential and productive. Next, we take every opportunity to find the beauty of silence, extracting the noise sources from our daily life. Lastly, we minimize the number of people we allow into our life, allowing ourselves to build quality into the important relationships.

Keep in mind these three enemies remain ready and waiting for the next victim. Ignorance is the bedrock of ineffectiveness. Forgetfulness is only a step away from the track that takes us back to ignorance. Of course, there is the laziness that summons, encourages and empowers the other culprits. This negligence removes the processes of continued learning and strips away and eliminates what has become a faltering commitment to sobriety. Laziness, forgetfulness and ignorance, each support and strengthen the growth of addictive behavior.

Take up the tools of sobriety that are directly opposed to these. Awareness of God through prayer and learning how to meditate on what is good and important. Establish an ongoing inventory of your spiritual condition and maintain daily spiritual fitness. Purposely and with intent, place yourselves in the path of those in need of freedom from addiction. Giving what we have will keep knowledge alive, memory active and apathy at bay.

One last thought on this matter. There are large numbers of people that are trapped in the ignorance of their personal addiction. Your diligence in maintaining sobriety positions your life to be an open book, to be read by those who are looking for freedom. Forgetting this fact, we slide into the abyss of laziness. Not only do we fail to share our life-giving story, timidity steps in and we find ourselves feeling that what we have to share is of no real value.

All the while, we applaud ourselves because we haven't drank or used. Virtue gets all the credit, as sobriety slowly fades and disappears into the old patterns of behavior that set us up for addiction in the beginning.

THE DEPRESSED MAN

There's a man sitting at a bar staring into his drink. He stays sitting like that for several hours. Later on this big wild looking biker, looking for trouble, steps up next to him.

He says to the man, "Hey, is that your drink?"

The man doesn't answer, so the biker grabs the drink from in front of the man and chugs it all down.

Rather than retaliating, the man just starts crying.

The biker says, "Come on man, I was just joking. Hey, how about I buy you another drink? I can't stand seeing a grown man cry!»

"No, it's not the drink", the man says. "This day has to be the worst one of my entire life. This morning I overslept, didn't hear the alarm and was late to my office. I try to explain but the owner refuses to listen and fires me. When I head out into the parking lot, I can't find my car, and then find out somebody stole it. The police finally show up and say they can do nothing".

"I called my insurance company and my policy had been cancelled for non-payment. I took an Uber to go home and when he pulls away, I discover I left my wallet with my money and credit cards."

"I tried to stop him, but the driver just keeps on going. I go into my house where I find my wife in bed with my best friend."

"So I leave home and walk to this bar. I have been sitting here thinking about just ending it all, when you show up and drink my poison."

CHAPTER 9

SOBRIETY ACCUMULATION VALUE

THERE ARE THOSE WHO WOULD say that the amount of time you are sober really doesn't matter. They will toss out the idea that it's the quality of sobriety, not quantity that makes a difference. Most of the time these are folks that are newly sober and are simply ashamed of the idea they have so little sobriety time. The shame is rooted in the grandiose thinking that they know a lot about sobriety and all about how to stay sober.

Others, who have some length of time sober that subscribe to the idea that time doesn't matter, say it out of feigned humility. They have distorted the true understanding of humility and refuse to allow any credit for the personal effort it takes to stand in faith and persevere year after year. This is a discredit to them and creates a devaluation of long-term sobriety in general.

Sobriety accumulation value represents the length of time a person has been clean and sober, and the value that they place on it. Simply put, the longer I'm sober, the more valuable my sobriety becomes. The longer I'm sober, the more the my life has accumulated value and control. The longer I'm sober, the more relationships I have and the more I cherish these relationships. The longer I'm sober the more I have built possessions in my life, and the less amount of control they have on me. The longer I'm sober the more tools I have to help other people. The longer I'm sober, the greater the spiritual dynamic that I live in.

Simply put, the longer I'm sober, the more valuable my sobriety becomes.

It becomes clear that sobriety accumulation value must have its foundation a real time measurement of how long I've been in recovery. Physically free from alcohol and drugs, mentally separated from the obsession, emotionally balanced and developing in connectional maturity. Not the least of these is, being spiritually grounded in what I believe.

The attempts to minimize the value of accumulated sobriety is particularly dangerous to the newcomer. A higher value should be placed on staying sober a week. When you couldn't stay sober for one day or even 12 hours, a whole week is a long time.

When you realize that after 30 years of hard drinking you have 30 days totally alcohol free, what an accomplishment! The 90-day mark has always been significant. When I made my first attempt at sobriety in 1973, they were big on the milestone of the 90-day window. The entire understanding of Post-Acute Withdrawal, that we now have, is linked to that 90 days sober timeframe.

They measured links of sobriety and celebrated when the person had first started off, had achieved 90 days, and then the tremendous one-year mark. They called it the birthday or anniversary and had a celebration cake. Many who had a home-group found the tradition was also extended to you, that you get up for the first time and tell your story. It was a voluntary requirement type event.

The person who has frequently relapsed will find it difficult to look at length of sobriety. I call those that have gone out and come back multiple times for multiple years, experienced beginners. They still carry much of the regret, remorse, and embarrassment of their frequent failures. These are part of the length of time doesn't matter folks. We help overcome those negative memories by celebrating the great accomplishments of staying sober.

So where does the cutoff come between celebrating the great victories of time accumulation and that the length of time doesn't matter? How do we navigate from one end of the spectrum to the other? Who started this and why?

Quality vs Quantity

This has become a standard argument presented by the time doesn't matter crowd. They seem to surmise that the two terms are mutually exclusive. That the importance of one excludes the other. If you have quality, the quantity doesn't matter. If you have quantity, then somehow you are void of the quality, they of course claim to possess. Both are vitally important.

The longer we are in recovery, the greater our testimony becomes. It is not a bragging right of how important we are, but a documentation of the reality that sobriety works. The evidence is that anyone can change, and not just in a fleeting way. Long term sobriety is an attestation that is loaded with evidence, that this works and can be permanent. For some, even the word permanent sends them cowering into retreat. They seem to believe that should they say they have recovered or found permanent sobriety, they are destined to lose it.

I hear that repeated frequently, "I'm only one drink away from a drunk".

"Nobody is safe from the next drink", even the famous, "You only have today, you might be drunk tomorrow, you never know". I get the premise. I know without any doubt if I were to start drinking or using drugs, I would be off to the races. Perhaps never stopping again.

I'm not in fear that I will accidentally pick up.

However, the truth is this. The longer I'm sober, and the more I have learned, the stronger my program becomes. Does that mean I forget about the basics? No, of course not. However, I am not afraid of a relapse. I'm not in fear that I will accidentally pick up. I am not concerned that getting healthier and building years into my sobriety somehow makes me more vulnerable. It is a counterpoint that does not make sense. Something like saying the better I get, the worse I become.

I have found that quality comes along with quantity. The longer I am at this, the better my understanding. The better my understanding, the clearer the pitfalls. The clearer I can see the pathway, the more likely it is that I will be clean and sober permanently. So, let me break down some aspects of long-term sobriety for the sake of demonstrating and substantiating it's affects and benefits.

What Constitutes Quality

It starts with being physically free from addiction. Now for me, it has been 40 years of experiencing this. Not to say that I have not been tempted, thought of the possibility or considered that I might not need to worry about it any longer.

But let me ask, "Where did the idea start that people cannot get free from addiction? Who relegated those coming out of addiction as permanently damaged, with no hope of finding permanent recovery? Who said that the best a person can hope for is to hold on with white knuckle tenacity, and hope somehow they will make it another day without being overpowered by addiction taking over again?"

This is a weak description of sobriety and has not been proven, at least in my way of thinking, to be true. People do get better. They do recover. They find a wonderful life, permanently free from addiction.

The only caveat is one simple rule. Don't take the first one. No matter what, stay away from the first drink, the first pill, the first bet, the first whatever. Once the first one is allowed in, there is no stopping the rest. The train comes down the track. It is true that nobody who has been run over by a train, has been hit by the caboose. It is the engine that makes the first hit every time and it causes most of the damage.

So, armed with this piece of information, relapsing into addiction can be permanently avoided, here's how. Remove the idea of consuming alcohol or drugs from your life. It is no longer part of the equation. It is not part of the question and never part of the answer. Life may get very difficult, throwing you the proverbial curve ball that is impossible to hit. However, your current life problem is not in any way connected to the idea of a drink or a substitute. The challenges cannot be solved by engaging an addiction. Should I return to old destructive behaviors is not the question. If it is not part of the question, then it is not part of the answer.

I don't have a drinking problem, I don't drink.

I have spent a considerable amount of time in a beautiful community where, because of their religious beliefs, the men wear turbans. They are different colors and sizes, unique in their wrapping style, and the men are diligent in this custom. As a side note, they are friendly, appear to be hard working, family men who are dedicated to their faith.

I have often thought, especially on the hotter days, do they ever get up and say, "I just don't want to wear this turban today" I may one day ask someone, but for now, it is just an observational type question.

The point for me is this. I have never one time in my entire life, gotten up in the morning and said, "I wonder if I should wear a turban today?" It is not part of my life. Never part of the question of the day; never part of a solution. It has never crossed my mind. It is a non-issue.

So it now is with alcohol and drugs. They are for me a non-issue. I don't have a drinking problem, I don't drink. Keeping myself from the re-entry of this active addiction into my life requires a transformation of thought and belief. I no longer believe that I am a helpless victim of the tyrannical rule of the mighty dictator we call addiction.

The days of cosmetic repair to those battling with addictions has faded. We can either get well, recover from the delusion that we are helpless, or perpetually live on the fearful edge of relapse.

So, can I stay physically free from addiction? Yes, if I choose to. Not only free from the substance, I can, as so many have done, get healthy. The right food intake, exercise regimen and medical advice can go a long way to conquering the physical side of addiction. Quality physical sobriety is a wonderful way to proceed into the other aspects of a sober life.

Mental Sobriety

What about being mentally separated from the obsession? Again, the answer would be yes. We become what we think about. So, what do you focus your day to day thoughts on? What are you feeding your mind?

If you watch nothing but violent movies, eventually you will become desensitized to the very acts of violence. When I was growing up, we watched the 3 Stooges. They hit, smacked, poked, pulled hair and called each other names. We laughed at it, while our parents were appalled at the violence. The old westerns had gunfights where someone always died. However, it was passive compared to the offerings of today. Graphic violence sells; cutting off limbs or heads, blood and gore presented in such and aggressive portrayal, that you might at some point need to turn away.

In general, our society has become more violent and aggressive. We have accepted it as the new normal. Anesthetized to the horror that it represents. The point is that we have fed our minds with images that have created an acceptance of what was once to us unacceptable.

The thought of using drugs or drinking, reactivating that terrible cycle of personal destruction and fear once again, is for most who are in comfortable sobriety, repulsive. However, should we entertain the idea of a cool beer on a hot summer afternoon, or smoking a little pot with some funny friends, our thinking may become out of touch with the reality.

So what do you think about? What runs through your mind repeatedly? You will find the value of having your mind free from the thoughts of your drug of choice if you simply feed your thoughts with positive images of not using. Once we are mentally free from the obsessive thoughts, a sober life becomes easy to access.

Emotionally Balanced

An essential part of sobriety is being emotionally balanced. Essential to emotional balance is connectional maturity. Who we are linked to emotionally is the core question. Securing an emotional stability that we are not too sad or not too happy, just ok, is much easier when we live separate from everyone. But the necessity to be connected to others brings the greater challenge. They have their own emotions and needs just like you.

So finding the balance in our feelings requires we enter the process of knowing our emotions, our likes and dislikes, our tolerances and triggers. I basically had two emotions that I could identify in the early days of sobriety. Anger and fear. If I had remained in the experience of this limited understanding, I would have found no quality in my sober life.

Today I have the entire range of emotions and know it is ok to feel everything. This fosters a freedom to interchange with others on a deeper level. No longer controlled by my emotions, I can experience life the way it was designed to be. This is quality.

Spiritually Grounded

Not the least of the characteristics of a quality sober life is being spiritually grounded. Firmly planted in what I believe and why I believe it. I no longer find it necessary to agree with everyone in what they believe. No longer need to debate the various points of my spiritual life.

As a Christian Believer, I have found a freedom in my relationship with God that supersedes my fear of what you might think of me. You are allowed to disagree with me and have your own beliefs and I do need not be offended. I tell people they don't have to believe what I believe, they have the right to be wrong.

The quality of my spiritual life came into realization when I stopped trying to believe everything and became comfortable in my own beliefs without apology. I found for me that trying to believe in everything, ultimately lead me to believe in nothing.

Maybe you have arrived at a juncture in time that requires another look at this matter. It will take a bit of self-determination, a break from faulty beliefs and some down to earth faith, in order to actually foster the necessary change to permanently break the cycle of addiction. But it can be done. It will require personal choice and a buy-in at the very basic level of human emotion, thought, and belief, in order to bring about the necessary change.

The Value of Accumulation

Quality sobriety is available. But it is not likely to happen on every level without accruing some actual time. Quality of your sobriety is actually included as a benefit to having gained quantity. What is it that makes long-term sobriety so valuable and increasing in value the longer I'm sober? Good question.

Here are 7 Value Points to Consider

1. Hope for Others

Those that see the long-term sober people can only surmise that, if it worked for that man and continues to, there is hope for me.

2. Valuing my Past

My past life of active addiction is a virtual wasteland. That is until I share it with others. The longer I'm sober the more opportunities I encounter to share my journey.

3. Commitment to Independence

Nothing will strip away the confidence others have in you than for you to relapse. The longer I remain free from addiction, the more I experience a sense of independence. Independence is freedom but it always comes at a cost. There is an old adage "Break a big rule and you will get lots of little rules". Retuning got addiction is the big rule. When you break it, freedom is soon swallowed up in many small rules you will need to follow.

4. Stability in Difficult Times

The tremendous lessons I have gained during hard times are a treasure that cannot be purchased. Having survived great life ordeals and coming out on the other side still sober, has produced a confidence that cannot be gained by observation or explanation.

5. Potential to Serve Others

We get better at helping others. Interchanging with thousands of people for decades, has given me more insight into the challenges newcomers have. With this acumen, comes a sensitivity and, at times, shrewd ability to find the right words on the right occasion.

6. Honoring Those Who Have Taught Me

Woe to me if I should ever forget the men and women who have taken part in my education and development. When I forget those who have helped me, I not only lose my gratitude, but also my perspective. If I forget who rescued me in my hour of need, I may forget those who need a helping hand now. Forget who brought me our and I may forget where I came from.

7. The Pathway to a God Connection

My life demonstrates on an increasing scale the vast miracle that God has worked in me. It was no small miracle that I ever found a sober life. The greater miracle is that the God who saved me from the destruction, has kept me over all these years. My connection to God has grown and my platform to declare his goodness has grown as well. God has given us the dispensation to overstate his greatness, generosity and love.

Conclusion

Surrender is essential before permanent change will be accessed. Exposure to the educational process of recovery is a good start but is only the entry point. Long term sobriety actually and always increases in value.

The company had been around for a long time and the board of directors felt it was time for a shakeup, so they hired a new CEO. The new leader was known as a tough boss and she wanted to live up to her reputation. She was determined to clear the company of all the dead weight. Out to identify those who were not putting in a good effort, she called on the general manager to tour the company with her.

On a tour of the facilities, the CEO came into a room full of workers. She wanted to let them know that she meant business. Seeing a young fellow leaning against the wall doing nothing, she decided to make an example of him.

She asked him, "Just how much money do you make a week?"

A little surprised, the young man looked at her and said,

«Well, I make $300 a week."

The determined CEO said, "Wait right here."

She went back to her office and a couple moments later reappeared.

She handed the guy $1,200 in cash, looked him in the eye and said, "Here's four weeks' pay. Now GET OUT and don't come back."

Feeling pretty good about the lesson she had taught everyone, she looked around the room and yelled, "Does anyone want to tell me what that lazy bum did here?"

From across the room a voice said, "That was the pizza delivery guy from Domino's."

Guess it pays to work at Domino's!

CHAPTER 10

SPIRITUAL STRENGTH

Everybody is looking for something.

SO HERE I AM IN Lynden, Washington in the middle of August and it is in the high 60s today. Seeing how the rest of the country is in a heatwave, it is notable.

In many ways, Lynden is like dropping back in time. A community built around dairy farms, blueberry, and raspberry fields, where everyone knows everyone or is at least friendly to everyone. This little town, where there is a church on every street and no real taverns, is situated about 5 minutes from the border crossing to Canada. On Sunday, most of the stores are closed and family seems to be the focus no matter what you are doing.

I recently attended the Great Northwest Washington Fair in Lynden. This event is about family. Children are everywhere and, as fairs go, it is clean and pleasant. From the afternoon horse shows to the demolition derby, it is all about the family doing this together.

Amidst the vast animal barns, (more than you could believe) and buildings filled with displays from collections to home-made baked goods and food, mostly home grown, is a little stage area that provides entertainment of all sorts. Singers, comedians (family friendly), jugglers and the like, filled with pithy humor and good fun. You can pass time under the giant shade trees, eat wonderful BBQ and homemade pie. Most of the time you can easily find a seat during the show, as people casually stroll in and out.

One event that is different is the Hypnotist Show. In most ways, it is like any other fair side show with the exception that it is packed for every show, 3 times a day. Every seat is full, people are sitting on the ground and there is standing room only around the outside of the bleacher style seating. Most shows on this stage have 150 or so in attendance, but this hypnotist has 300 or more for every show.

What is the draw? Something beyond the natural and explainable. It doesn't matter if their perception is that it is real or fake, people are drawn to the supernatural. Consider the Harry Potter craze. In this sleepy little town where there is a church on every corner, the desire for something supernatural is still huge!

Are you aware that a large portion of the society we live in, not just in Lynden, are drawn to and are even actively looking for something supernatural? People want something real! Something that they can see, feel, touch or experience.

So it is with the addicted. Before the addiction, there was a void that we were looking to fill. We grabbed anything and everything to fill the void. But we discovered that once we were clean and sober, the void didn't go away. Nothing in the natural can fill this void. The supernatural is needed and sought out.

A short-lived side show event will never fill the need. A concept of God or the statement that I believe in God won't either. For those trying to break the cycle of addiction, the supernatural intervention of a personal God is all that will ever satisfy the void. Never settle for a sleight of hand spirituality, when you can have the real thing.

I must confess, I have always been a believer in Jesus; I grew up that way. I was taught the Bible from a young age, and honestly, I cannot remember a time when I thought about becoming an unbeliever. I have always been a believer, but not always a follower.

I have always been a believer, but not always a follower.

There were many years when I followed what I wanted, my own self will. I believed on some level but had no faith. I believed there was a God and understood the stories about Jesus. But I had no faith to be able to put any of it into practice.

How do we move faith from passive belief to engagement? That has been and still is for many the question. Here are some ideas that explain this faith we so desperately need.

What is faith? What does it look like?

1. Faith is speaking and acting like something has changed before it is evident.
2. Faith is finding hope to achieve that which is unattainable.
3. Faith is believing in the dream that has eluded you but not yet died.
4. Faith is seeing God feed the birds on the beach by washing minnows from the sea.

Faith and trust go hand in hand. There is an old story about a man at Niagara Falls getting ready to push a wheelbarrow across the falls on a tight-wire. The man who was attempting this daring maneuver said to an onlooker, "Do you have faith I can cross the falls on the tight-wire pushing this wheelbarrow?"

The onlooker said, Why yes, I do." The man pushing the wheelbarrow said,

"Do you trust I can make it?"

The onlooker said, "Yes, I trust you will make it."

The man pushing the wheelbarrow said, "If you trust, then get in the wheelbarrow, and ride it across."

Saying you trust is different than actually trusting.

What is Trust? What Does It Look Like?

1. Trust is speaking and acting like someone has your best interests before it is evident.
2. Trust is a risk successfully survived.
3. Trusting a person requires placing confidence in their motives. Sometimes they think their motives or actions are right, but they are not.
4. Trust is easier when motives are based on principles.

To be told to trust God, trust your family, trust those in your workplace, even trust the AA people, is a tall order for someone just getting sober. Trusting them is only part of the equation. The next step is gaining their trust in you. Real trust is formulated in a relationship only when it becomes a mutual experience.

Keep in mind that no human power; not groups, sponsors, counselors, therapists, or even churches, can relieve an addiction. We're told to trust the process, but without God's power, it cannot bring wholeness. These all can help to place one in a position to stay spiritually connected, but in and of themselves, they provide no permanent relief.

We want to trust that God is good and will never leave us or let us down, yet sometimes we won't bank our lives on this for fear of disappointment. When we are challenged to believe, we resist believing at the most crucial time. In the place where we have the greatest need to believe and often where we most want to believe, we find our heart resisting.

This doesn't just happen. Somewhere between a desire to believe and the fear of believing, there is a hesitation. Old wounds, resentments over religious training, or false beliefs about those who claim to be believers but didn't act that way, will all cause us to resist. At the early stages of our needing and wanting to believe in God, the faith matter seems more desirable than credible.

Perhaps we are so apprehensive about believing what we want to believe, that we miss believing what we need to believe. But neither the desirability nor the credibility of the matter are the problem. What matters to the dubious seeker is that past hurts and failures remain hidden and effectively safeguarded. Here is the catch. These beliefs, that are quite desirable and perfectly credible must then be dismissed. When we feel deceived, the fear comes back and blocks our progress. Fear is always fueled by deception.

In presenting God to a newcomer we often err. When our approach is too aggressive, we discover that, in the very moment they need to be focused, we tend to try to force our faith on them. When we begin to impose and pressure them, our credibility is lost and unfortunately, so is their desire to believe. God has never imposed himself on me, why should I even think of trying to pressure someone into believing? If my relationship is right with God, they will desire to have that same kind of relationship. It is vastly more important to foster desire than to lose your credibility in vain attempts of forcing your faith on them.

Their denial is a form of self-preservation that protects them from looking directly at the truth. If we carefully examine their deeply held, underlying assumptions, we will see that their resistance is fostered by fear. Much of the time, their emotions will clearly disclose and expose what they wish to suppress or fear to verbalize.

So it is with these new to the faith message. The desire to believe becomes a stronger force than the fear; fear that is based on a lack of trust. Their desire to know about God and faith is buffered by this lack of trust. Our zeal to help may diminish our credibility. Not until desirability becomes greater than credibility, will they truly believe.

This is not always a moral dialogue between the voices of right and wrong; sometimes it is a desperate deliberation between hope and fear. Hope of reward and fear of consequences. The process is stymied by attempting to hold two opposing views. “I need to be honest, but I’m afraid. I hope to find wellness, but I’m afraid of the consequences.” (Consequences that are either real or perceived.) I know it is wrong, but I want it anyway. This is known as cognitive dissonance.

Cognitive Dissonance

Cognitive dissonance is simultaneously holding two conflicting beliefs. If we stop there long enough, ambivalence will set in. If we continually experience the feeling of the two conflicting emotions simultaneously, we will become disillusioned, disappointed, and frustrated. This is a common state to find yourself in at the beginning of your spiritual journey. If you don’t find a clear path your destined to stay stuck spiritually.

The reason we stay spiritually weak is a matter of not finding a clear direction for our faith.

We Stay Spiritually Weak When We Are:

Misguided Not knowing what to believe.

Misinformed Not knowing how to live spiritual principles.

Misdirected Creating our own rules.

Mis-motivated Living in apathy.

Miscalculation Giving in to temptations or personal wants.

Mis-aligned Empty spiritual reserves. Hand to mouth empowerment.

Having faith is the answer. However, uncertainty of what to believe remains the challenge. How do we get faith when we have doubt?

Faith is not a predisposition to force every piece of supporting information to fit into the mold of one's belief; that is science. If I can calculate and measure every component of my belief system, to have the ability to rationally make it all work, it is a belief system void of faith altogether.

God makes himself and His purposes known to us partially and sequentially. Knowing that God has a plan for any of my life situations, brings freedom and confidence. His will for my life is a progressive and unfolding revelation. The patterns of a self-driven life are voided in the light of his love, which is revealed in his plan.

Faith in God is actually easy to understand. Faith is - - -

1. Not discussing God's will, but doing God's will.
2. Not trying to explain God as much as believing God.
3. Not trying to understand God as much as trusting God.
4. Not trying to pressure others with God but holding out a welcoming hand.

Early in my recovery, I was full of zeal and full of myself and quite sure I knew the answer to this spiritual melee. I wanted to tell everyone what I had discovered and how they too could have what I had. Interestingly, not many wanted whatever it was that I had. I was just a bit too eager and it was a bit too egotistical.

My sponsor saw both the good and the not so good in my desire to help others find God. He gave me a little illustration that helped me as it were, "land the plane".

He said, "Hold out your hand". Then he said, "If you were to put some bird seed on your hand and sit really still, and if you waited motionless long enough, a bird would come and eat the seed right out of your hand. They would be comfortable eating there as long as you were still and didn't startle them."

"However, if you waited until the bird was eating and suddenly closed your hand to try to force the bird to stay on your hand, the bird would fight to get away."

He said, "If you just hold truth out for anyone to come and take what they want, they will always feel comfortable and come back for more. You can't force anyone to believe".

Whenever I would get a little too forceful, Walt my sponsor, would hold out his hand, smile and say, "Just wait".

Faulty Belief Systems

Personal freedom has become the lord of many lives. The more freedom we have in personal choice, the more it rules over our life.

When we begin our journey, God is a very small part of our life. We recognize the need for God; however, we are quite resistant to any such talk. Often this is based on our prior experience with people trying to force feed us a connection to God. Their well-intentioned efforts are based on their desire to help us resolve our problems.

For the most part, we have entered a mindset I call "spiritual resistance". My personal observation is that God never forces himself on anyone. Those who come in the name of God, with an overbearing approach most often turn people off rather than engaging them in a life changing solution.

Suffice it to say, particularly at the beginning, God holds a very small place in the life of the person newly coming into recovery. It commonly starts with saying, "I'm spiritual, not religious" Kind of a backwards approach to believing in God. Saying I'm spiritual appears on the surface to be more palatable and inclusive; perhaps a little less threatening and daunting. I can be spiritual and not have to concern myself with those who do not understand my brand of oddity. This seems to diminish confrontation and the need for defending one's self is obliterated when there are no right or wrong delineations of belief.

Eventually the seeker, who is you, will conclude deep in your heart that you believe in God. That God has somehow miraculously intervened in your life to remove your addiction. At the same time, as you accept faith to believe in God, you reject the basic understanding of God which millions of people have had for centuries. You have instead decided to make up some idea about God and recovery from addiction, unique to you alone.

Suddenly, as though struck from above, some how you are right, and the rest of society is wrong. You must be among some of the most brilliant people who have ever stood on the planet. To actually believe that you're right and everyone else is wrong is a clear demonstration of self-centeredness and pride. This is the notion that man can create a God who is more powerful than themselves. It does not meet the threshold of commonsense.

Trying to enlarge your spiritually you formulate a series of rituals and routines that make you feel very spiritual. Some of this is real and based on our faith. Some not so much. These rituals actually mean something, at least to us. Going through the motions, adhering to actions and activities that make us feel spiritual or lucky (as odd as they sometimes may seem), is a religious experience in and of itself.

These rituals actually mean something, at least to us.

So, suspend cynical reasoning for just another moment. What is wrong with religious practice? It seems exclusionary, mystical on some level, inexplicable to the onlooker, impossible to understand unless you have the revelation, which is personal. Revelation is not revelation unless it is your revelation. So, who can judge when you have your very own basket of routines, that hold special meaning to you?

Religion and religious practice are not limited to the organized church. Recovery meetings are replete with rituals that certainly appear odd to the observer. Fishermen have rituals, athletes do, fans do, actors certainly do, and the list goes on. Even drunks and addicts cling to rituals.

My belief is the biggest part of the decision I make regarding recovery from addiction. When I started my recovery and I asked God for help. I wanted a definitive connection with God and I wanted a God guard my life, mainly so I would avoid stepping back into the addiction and the trouble that came with it. To believe that God has freed me from active addiction says a lot about my decision.

No matter what it means to you or what your specific beliefs are, we are certainly better off trying to be connected to God. There is a verse that says He has brought us out of darkness into his great light. Maybe I didn't find God, but he found me. If God found me and rescued me, it would seem logical that I would want to get to know everything I can about this loving God.

When we choose to reject any outside established understanding of God, we will automatically form a failing belief system. Why is this true? Because we are broken people and most everything we believed has failed so far. The likelihood that this has or will just change is not reality. So, let's review some of the characteristics of a dysfunctional belief system.

Faulty Belief Systems:

1. A power greater than you that you create, is actually a power lesser than you.
2. A God that is exclusive to me, must not be working in others, just me.
3. The belief that my failure is planned, but that my defects are not removed but are put on hold just to return again and again.
4. A belief that there is no basis for forgiveness because we cannot judge right or wrong; it is all about how I feel. After all, forgiveness requires that we establish right and wrong and a moral plumb-line.
5. Only learning about and knowing God through an educational process. No Divine intervention or revelation moment, or born-again experience.
6. God designs a pathway for us to live a spiritual life, but our spiritual growth is primarily formulated from on-going suffering. How can such an intrinsically flawed design come from a loving God?

Spiritual Priorities

There are only two things you need to stay sober. Don't drink and change your entire life. Our time and affection were all devoted to our addiction. This must change and frankly, any change is likely to be good. To find spiritual strength, we must put our life in order. Without alignment of all aspects of our life, we will remain dysfunctional even after we become real spiritual.

It would seem that for many, the top priority becomes the process of recovery itself. Recovery meetings, recovery talk, recovery books, and all things recovery. Recovery thinking will dominate their world. For the newcomer the first level of priority will now be addiction recovery. Kept in balance, this will activate the change process. It becomes quite necessary for building a foundation for permanent recovery. But what about your other priorities?

For some, the connection with God starts to take precedence across-the-board. They have recognized that without God's intervention and empowerment, all of the other things they try are futile. This is now, and will be in the future, the most valuable lesson that they could learn in life. However balance is necessary to maintain a healthy life.

For them, if there's a benefit in becoming addicted and now being sober, it is finding freedom through God which certainly is a benefit. Their priority will likely become this connection with God. A deliberate approach to forming and building a connection with God becomes something that they will devote both time and energy to.

This may, for a season, become such a high priority that development of other areas is neglected. It is good that understanding your connection to God has improved, but perspective is needed. This is where the saying started, "They are so heavenly minded they are no earthly good". A mismanagement of priorities.

So they look at the family. If there is an area of life that has been neglected on a wider scale than that of our relationship with God, it would be our relationship and efforts with our family. People in addiction frequently fail at financially supporting their family; they overlook the importance of personal goals and the personal achievements of other members of the family, and for the most part, they remain emotionally unavailable.

Consciousness of the damage that's been caused to the family by their neglect increases. So, they will reprioritize their family to a higher level. Often at the beginning, not so much out of virtue but out of fear of losing whatever relationship they may have left. The importance of being a husband or a wife coupled with the value and necessity of being a good parent becomes obvious.

It becomes increasingly clear just how important their family is to them. This is a major factor in a happy life. It includes time with their spouse rekindling their romance and renewing their commitment to their marriage. They will begin listening to their children and connecting to their activities and desires, both educationally and socially.

It is not long until they see the in attention to the extended family; this also becomes more of a priority. They become aware that they could be a great support for putting your life back together. Making time to connect with extended family becomes a normal part of this new structure.

Blessed are the flexible, for they shall not be bent out of shape.

Soon they see that having done such a poor job of keeping family as a priority, financial obligations are now very high. The natural tendency is to try to make up for lost time. Not only in paying the bills but they become aware that they could lose their job if they don't straighten up. Many times, legal consequences and other areas neglected make the mountain of money obligations seem even bigger.

This is when they need to look at their job situation. The decisions and choices they made to ignore their employment, or even career options, have put them at risk. This negligence was part of their active addiction. For most employment, even entry-level type jobs, was difficult.

They found getting into trouble with the boss was frequent. Many have been through continuous employ woes that caused them to move from job to job. Trouble with the law also jeopardize their employment. Missed days, poor performance often ended the tenure, or minimally blocked the possibility of moving forward in the company.

Quickly this becomes such high priority, after all without money you cannot care for your family. So the family may get moved down the list once again to fall in line behind employment. In the alignment of priorities, finances seem to take the lead. In its rightful place employment is a vital part of a healthy life. We may have been neglectful in this area in times past, but now we have stabilized our current employment and established it as a high priority.

We don't live to work, we work to live.

The manner in which we accumulate resources to fund our life often receives the most attention, the most time, and the most energy. It seems that we build the rest of our life around our employment. After all, if we are to care for our family, keep our house in order and have some resources left over for fun activities, we will need to work.

Often, we have seen that the person will try to make up for lost time. They become consumed with making money and the other priorities get lost in the mix. Remember, we don't live to work, we work to live.

So the priorities of making recovery meetings, having a spiritual life, and the commitment of spending time with our families begins to slide to second and third place.

Some other oversights that need attention include, care for your physical body. This has likely been a missing component for many. Without a focus on diet and exercise, the other areas of life become negatively impacted. This needs to be a focus, but again, excess may lead to neglect in some other area of life. We need to be healthy so we can work and care for our family. Must be a priority.

What about fun? The hobbies and extracurricular activities? They have dropped to the bottom of the priority list for most out of necessity. There is now little time or resources left over for anything. Recovery from addiction, financial recovery and restructuring the family leaves little time for anything else. The lack of resources also sets extracurricular activities way down the list. However, it is really important to have a little fun time, so you fit it in.

These activities that we enjoy create a balanced sense of well-being. So reclaiming your favorite hobby or activity is vital. This is the thing that they you to do best, fishing, sports, even working out. So we take some time away from taking care of the place where we live and the things we have that makes it a home. This becomes a higher priority than some of the other items already covered.

So we started off with the importance of a spiritual foundation, then caring for our family and extended family, then the employment, then fun and then our house. So as important as all these things are, likely you won't get all of them on the priority, something will be left out.

So go back to the active drinking days, when all of it was neglected. Before you feel you must accomplish everything that is now obvious, remember that the neglect has been there for a long time. You won't be able to fix it all at once. If everything is a high priority, ultimately nothing finds first place. Slowly but surely you will rebuild your life, but take it one step at a time.

Finding a sustainable balance is an absolute necessity. I have listed some variables below when we should neglect one area or another.

5 Basic Spiritual Priorities

1. Recovery processes without God are ineffective. So our first priority becomes to daily make the connection with God and take time to focus on our spiritual life.

2. A relationship with God, without the recovery processes, become hyper-spiritual. So a second priority must be active participation in a recovery group and with a sponsor. This will allow you to have a spiritually grounded recovery program. Without it nothing else works.
3. A spiritually grounded recovery program, without appropriate family care, becomes self-centered. So the third priority is your family. They must have access to some of your time and attention. However, keep in mind that building a healthy family without a spiritually grounded recovery program, will end up in dysfunction.
4. Having a God centered program and building a healthy family unit without an income, becomes very stressful and is irresponsible. So priority number four is to get a sustainable job, and build a budget. Too much of a focus on money cause neglect of the spiritually grounded recovery program and your family.
5. Get some balance in what you do. The process of recovery remains a high priority because recovery becomes interwoven with every part of our life. Our relationship with God, our family connection and even our work, all depend on it. Attendance at meetings, embracing the step process and eventually helping others all become part of the picture.

The necessary alignment of priorities, while improved, is not permanent by any means. Let's move a year into recovery and see what the priorities look like at that point. They may not be the exactly the same but the basics will still be there. If we have made progress, we will discover the need to readjust ourselves to meet the increased responsibilities and obligations.

A sober life demands that we have flexibility because, like it or not, our priorities change. You know the old saying, Blessed are the flexible, for they shall not be bent out of shape.

Once you have been sober for a while, working the steps, connecting with God, and straightening out your family, you will see that this process is doable. Understand that at first it may seem overwhelming. So always be willing to see where you are out of alignment in your priorities and adjust without complaint.

A couple of last thoughts on Spiritual Strength:

- If I take a drink, all bets are off. So you must stay sober.
- If I put anything before my sobriety, it will be the second thing I'll lose.
- If I ignore my connection with God, my family is next.
- If I ignore my family, my connection with God is likely to shrink as well.

COMMON TERMINOLOGY USED IN ADDICTIONS/RECOVERY

Abstinence: A total removal from alcohol and drug use.

Acetaminophens: Pain relievers (e.g. Tylenol) used to treat headaches, muscle aches, headaches, etc.

ACOA: Adult Children of Alcoholics. A support group for those with alcoholic parents.

Adderall: Is used to treat attention deficit hyperactivity disorder (ADHD) and narcolepsy, people use it illegally, due to the desired effects, a combination of amphetamine and dextroamphetamine, both of which are central nervous system stimulants. It helps with focusing and concentration, increased mood level. Street names are Dexies, Speed, Black beauties.

Addict: A common term describing a person addicted to drugs.

Addiction Assessment: The process used to evaluate the presence and level of a persons addiction. Measures include environment, mental health history, physical condition, employment and family.

Addiction Counselor: A person trained to assist clients with the process of recovery from addiction.

Addiction Treatment: A program, normally residential, where a person undergoes intensive teaching and or therapy to address addiction problems

Addiction: Behavior that is actively engaged overusing or abusing substances such as drugs, alcohol, food, or behaviors that have caused a person to lose the ability to control the frequency and outcomes of their actions.

Addiction Discursion: The process of discoursing or reasoning through a behavior. The process of systematically inventorying ones behaviors from active addiction to shame based issues.

Addictive Personality: A measured mental health condition that indicates the likelihood of the development of addiction.

Adverse Reaction: A detrimental reaction to a drug, which was not the expected result.

Age of Onset: The likely age when a persons addictive behavior was measurable.

Agonist: A drug that activates a receptor in the brain.

Ala-non: A support group for family member's or friend's that are dealing with the side effects of living with those suffering from addictions.

Alcohol addiction: Substance abuse disorder where one is addicted to alcohol. A progressive, chronic disease, that left untreated often results in death. Marked with attempts to control excessive drinking, binge drinking, preoccupation with drinking. Failure to stop or control this behavior are marked by legal challenges, personal and health, family and financial difficulties.

Alcoholics Anonymous (AA): A voluntary program focused exclusively with alcoholics helping other alcoholics find and maintain recovery and sobriety.

Alcoholism: Substance abuse disorder where one is addicted to alcohol. A progressive, chronic disease, that left untreated often results in death. Marked with attempts to control excessive drinking, binge drinking, preoccupation with drinking. Failure to stop or control this behavior are marked by legal challenges, personal and health, family and financial difficulties.

Alkaloids: Plant-produced organic compounds that are the active ingredients in many drugs.

Amphetamine: A behavioral stimulant. Known in common terms as speed, uppers or pep pills.

Analgesic: Medication designed to treat pain.

Antagonist: A substance that can cancel the effects of other drugs.

Aspirin: An anti-inflammatory agent used for pain relief.

Authorized Character Defects: This is giving myself permission to violate my own standards and participate in old behavior patterns. Permission is granted based on the false claim that I don't have the ability to control my behavior.

Barbiturate: A type of drug known as depressants. When taken as prescribed, barbiturates help people with insomnia or with symptoms of anxiety.

Basic Text: The primary text of the Narcotics Anonymous (NA) organization. Modeled after the AA Big Book it explains the 12 Steps and 12 Traditions used in a addiction recovery program. Contains personal stories of recovery from active addiction.

Bath Salts: One of the newest drugs to hit the streets. They are called bath salts because they are usually packaged as a product "for a soothing bath, not for human consumption." Can produce euphoria and increased sociability and sex drive. Some users experience paranoia, agitation, and hallucinatory delirium, some display psychotic and violent behavior. Street names are Bloom, Cloud nine, Flakka, Scarface.

Benzodiazepine: A group of depressants used to induce sleep, prevent seizures, produce sedation, relieve anxiety and muscle spasms, etc.

Big Book: The primary text of the Alcoholics Anonymous organization. The AA Big Book explains the 12 Steps and 12 Traditions used in a addiction recovery program. Contains personal stories of recovery from active addiction.

Blood Alcohol Level: The measurable level of alcohol found in a persons blood.

Caffeine: A active stimulant found in coffee, tea and energy drinks.

Cannabis: A herbal drug that is made from the Cannabis plant. It contains chemicals called cannabinoids. Cannabinoids affect the central nervous system. Is smoked, taken orally, spray or added to foods. Street names are Mary Jane, Reefer, Pot, Weed, Bud, Herb. High medicinal qualities, but addictive and used primarily for the high.

Carcinogen: A cancer-causing chemical agent.

Causal Factors: Conditions that are conducive to individual chemical dependency problems. Physical condition, environment, genetics, mental health.

Caustic Fear: A fear that is abrasive, is bitter, cutting and corroding. It wears away resistance and destroys slowly without immediate impact or notice.

Ceiling Effect: When the dosage of drugs is increased beyond maximum levels, resulting in affect.

Cirrhosis: Chronic liver disease related to excessive alcohol consumption.

Closed Meetings: 12-Step meetings that are open only to individuals who have admitted they have an addiction or think that they may have, and are seeking help stopping.

Cocaine: Is a drug made from the leaves of the coca plant native to South America. A highly addictive stimulant, it increases alertness and energy. It affects the neuropathways in your brain, leading you to feel talkative, energetic, and euphoric. Addiction to cocaine can develop quickly, even after trying it only a few times. Street names are Coke, Snow, Powder, Blow.

Codeine: A mild pain-relieving sedative agent contained in opium. Street names, Schoolboy, Cody, Captain Cody.

Codependence: A behavioral addiction seen in family member's or friend's as the side effects from living with those suffering from addictions. Indicators are the act of taking responsibility for the addicted persons choices and allows the addict to avoid consequences of the addictive behavior.

Cold Turkey: To stop drinking or using a drug or a behavior abruptly or without gradual detoxification.

Compulsion: Frequently repeated behavior, done either knowingly or involuntarily.

Cognitive Dissidence: Wanting two or more of anything that are contradictory to one another.

Constituent Analyzation: This is taking other people's inventory. In doing so, we are making the presumption that we know all the facts and motives.

Crack: Crack cocaine, is a free base form of cocaine that can be smoked. Crack offers a short, intense high to smokers. It is the most addictive form of cocaine and users are often hooked after one use. Street names are Rocks, Nuggets, Hail.

Craving: The urgent desire to use a substance. Like a craving for a certain food.

Crisis Intervention: The action taken when one's usual coping resources pose a threat to individual or family functioning.

Disappointment Pathos: Is an emotion, a passion, or feeling of deep sadness. We have become disappointed and are suffering with disillusionment about people, circumstances and even disenchantment with our own beliefs.

Delayed Gratification: Resisting behaviors that produce an immediate reward in preference for a later reward.

Delirium Tremens: Alcohol withdrawal involving severe physical withdrawal symptoms, mental and emotional confusion, and hallucinations. This occurs in severely alcohol addicted individuals after they discontinue the use of alcohol.

Denial: Refusal or the inability to admit the reality of the amount or frequency of a person's using.

Depressants: Sedative drug that slows the rate of the body's functions. Includes alcohol.

Depression: A mood disorder that causes a persistent feeling of sadness and loss of interest.

Detoxification: The process for intentional removal of drugs or alcohol from the body. With or without medications or therapy.

Detox Center: A term used to describe the medical facility used to safely assist people coming off from drugs or alcohol.

Diminished Time Continuum Value: The lost ability to measure the amount of time wasted on that which is unproductive.

Dirty: Street term used to describe failing a urine test that is positive for drugs.

Disease Model: A theory of alcoholism that considers the addiction a disease rather than a social or psychological or spiritual issue.

Disease: A physical, mental or emotional condition, with medical symptoms that often have a known cause.

Displaced Regret: It is a sorrow that one feels and accepts as one's necessary portion in life, sentimental pessimism.

Doctor Shopping: Describes a patient requesting care from multiple physicians, in order to receive higher amounts of medications.

Dopamine: A neurotransmitter that plays a role in pleasure, motivation. Naturally produced by the body it is released by drug use.

Drinking or using dream: A dream during the recovery process that the person dreams they are drinking or using again. These are usually very realistic and fearful.

Dual-Diagnosis: An person addicted to substances who also is experiencing a mental health disorder.

DUI: Stands for driving under influence. Includes alcohol or another substance that impairs a persons ability to drive.

DWI: Stands for (driving while intoxicated).

Dysphoria: The emotional state of feeling very unhappy, uneasy, or dissatisfied. Can include anxiety, depression, or unease.

Elder Statesman: A person who has been sober a long time but is specifically known for the virtues their life demonstrates.

Enabling: Permitting an addicted person to continue in negative behaviors by providing support or assistance.

Endorphins: The body's opium-like substances produced in the brain to make a person happy, also natural painkillers.

Euphoria: A state of intense happiness, a feeling of well-being or elation, self-confidence, sometimes pathologically exaggerated.

Evidence-based Treatment: Treatment methods that have incremental indicators of success. Not exclusively connected to being clean and sober.

Exoneration Refusal: Clinging to unreasonable, obsolete grudges. Not forgiving when there appears a logical, sensible reason to do so.

Ecstasy: Psychoactive drug chemically similar to the stimulant methamphetamine and the hallucinogen mescaline. It is an illegal drug that acts as both a stimulant and psychedelic, producing an energizing effect, as well as distortions in time and perception and enhanced enjoyment from tactile experiences. Street names are Candy, Molly, Skittles.

Fentanyl: A synthetic opioid that is 80-100 times stronger than morphine. Pharmaceutical fentanyl was developed for pain management treatment of cancer patients, applied in a patch on the skin. Because of its powerful opioid properties, it is added to heroin to increase its potency, or be disguised as highly potent heroin, which often results in overdose deaths. Street names Apache, China white, Goodfella, TNT.

Fetal Alcohol Syndrome: Birth defects or abnormalities found in babies who's mother was actively using alcohol.

Fetal Drug Syndrome: Birth defects or abnormalities found in babies who's mother was actively abusing drugs.

Hallucinogen: Chemical substance that distorts perceptions, sometimes resulting in delusions or hallucinations.

Higher Power: A common term used to describe a belief in God. Used by those who are unsure of their beliefs.

Heroin: Processed from morphine, a naturally occurring substance extracted from the seedpod of the Asian poppy plant. Heroin usually appears as a white or brown powder. Used medically in several countries to relieve pain. Commonly used as a recreational drug for its euphoric effects. Street names are smack, junk, black tar, dragon, horse.

Hydrocodone: An opioid narcotic similar to heroin, and morphine used for pain. Risky because you can become addicted even when you are taking them as recommended by your doctor. Street names are Hydros, Tabs, Watsons, Loris, 357s.

Imminent Calamity: It is apprehension, uneasiness, restlessness, and some forms of disquiet. Something bad is going to happen, a sense of impending doom.

Increased tolerance: An expanded frequency in using that results in lower effect or diminished return.

Internalized Defiance: The unspoken protests that occur when we feel we are being told what to do, how to think or how to behave.

Illusion of control: The belief is that we control the outcomes by our repetitive thoughts.

Inhalant: Breathing in chemical vapors to produce a high. These include aerosols, gases, and solvents.

Intoxication: The condition of diminished mental or physical control as the result of the effects of alcohol or drugs.

Layered Denial: Denying not only the core issue, but ignoring the secretive maneuvers used to avoid facing the very challenges that highlight the fact that something is wrong.

Legal Drugs: Everyday drugs for medical use such as over the counter medications, prescription meds, alcohol, caffeine, nicotine.

LSD: Lysergic acid diethylamide, is a hallucinogenic drug that was first synthesized a Swiss scientist in the 1930s. During the Cold War, the CIA conducted clandestine experiments with LSD (and other drugs) for mind control, information gathering and other purposes. Over time, the drug became a symbol of the 1960s counterculture, eventually joining other hallucinogenic and recreational drugs at rave parties. Street names are Acid, Doss, Pane, Lucy, Golden dragon.

Maintenance drinking or using: Consuming alcohol or drugs in sufficient quantity to avoid withdrawal, but not appear to be limited or impaired.

Mania: A state of psychological and/or physiological hyperactivity generally lasting a week or longer. Characterized by euphoric mood, excessive activity and talkativeness, impaired judgment, and sometimes grandiose delusions.

Marijuana: A herbal drug that is made from the Cannabis plant. It contains chemicals called cannabinoids. Cannabinoids affect the central nervous system. Mostly smoked, orally, spray or added to foods. Street names are Mary Jane, Reefer, Pot, Weed, Bud, Herb. High medicinal qualities, but addictive.

Medical Marijuana: Used by the medical profession as a medicine for pain and symptoms of multiple sclerosis.

Medical Model: An addiction theory that categorizes addiction as disease rather than a moral deficiency.

Metabolism (of drugs): The breakdown and absorption of drugs by chemical and physical reactions of the body.

Methadone: A synthetically produced opioid often used to detox a person from heroin. Also used as a street drug that produces a high. Street names Dollies, Fizzies, Jungle juice, Metho.

Methamphetamine: A white crystalline drug is snorted, smoking or injecting it with a needle. It creates a false sense of happiness and well-being—a rush of confidence, hyperactiveness. A decreased appetite. Effects generally last from six to eight hours. Crank, Tweek, Crystal, Ice.

Mono-therapy: The use of a single drug to treat a particular disorder or disease.

Morphine: A major sedative/pain reliever found in opium.

Multi-leveled denial: Denial that not only ignores the core issue, but also the stimulus that compels our awareness of these challenges.

Naloxone: A medication used to block the effects of opioid overdose. It is known as Narcan, a brand name.

Narcotic: A drug that in moderate doses dulls the senses, relieves pain, and induces profound sleep but in excessive doses causes stupor, coma, or convulsions. High dependence risk.

Narcotics Anonymous AA: A voluntary program focused exclusively with addicts helping other addicts find freedom from drugs.

Narrowness of Opportunity: Losing the ability to consider other viable options do to obsessive thinking.

Negative Reinforcement: A form of learning change behaviors as to avoid unpleasant consequences. The person is rewarded for desired behavior by the removal of a negative consequence.

Neurotransmitter: A neurotransmitter is defined as a chemical messenger, as epinephrine or acetylcholine, that carry signals between nerve cells, and other cells in the body. These chemical messengers can affect a wide variety of both physical and psychological functions including heart rate, sleep, appetite, mood, and fear.

Neutralization of Emotions: Treating all experiences, people and feelings as equal. Numbing myself by not feeling reality.

Newcomer: a person who has just arrived at the recovery meetings. First meeting or week of meetings.

Nicotine: A chemical from a night shade plant, Normally smoked in cigarettes, it has a strong mood altering effects and can act on the brain as both a stimulant and a relaxant. It can lead to further drugs misuse also. It is harmful to the heart, lungs, arteries, and brain. It is a component valued as an insecticide. Tobacco use is extremely addictive.

Obsession: A mental process indicative of a intense desire or longing for someone or something. desire.that repeats the same thought continuously. Sometimes involuntarily can be harmful.

Obsessive planning: Believing that thinking about one thing over and over will cause it to change.

Obsessive Progressives: Those who obsessive thinking seems necessary for them to move forward, in even the smaller tasks.

Off-Label Use: Off-label use of pharmaceutical drugs indicates application for an unapproved malady or in an inappropriate age group, dosage, or route of administration.

Old Timer: Someone who has been clean and sober for over 25 years.

Opiate: Is a term classically used in pharmacology to mean a drug derived from opium.

Opioid: A more modern term for opiates. It is used to designate all such substances, both natural and synthetic.

Opium: The poppy's natural ingredients and their derivatives (opium, morphine, codeine, and heroin). One of the most popular drugs; contained in muscle-relaxers, sleeping pills, and tranquilizers.

Over-the-Counter Drugs: Legal non-prescription drugs. Sometimes used in an application not in accordance with manufactures recommendations for the purpose of getting high.

Oxycodone: A opioid oral tablet prescribed medication, that's used to treat moderate to severe pain. Highly addictive often abused and sold as a street drug referred to as Hillbilly Heroin, Blues, Kickers, Oxys, 512s,

PCP: A drug used for its mind-altering effects. PCP may cause hallucinations, distorted perceptions of sounds, and violent behavior. As a recreational drug, it is typically smoked, but may be taken by mouth, snorted, or injected. It may also be mixed with cannabis or tobacco. Street names are Angel dust, Ozone, Rocket fuel, Peter Pan, Embalming fluid.

Painkillers: A slang term describing analgesic substances, opioids and non-opioids.

Percocet: A painkiller that's part of a family of drugs known a opioids it is synthesized in a lab, it is the brand name of a drug that mixes oxycodone and acetaminophen. Can create a sense of euphoria and numb pain, but they can also slow breathing. Street names Percs, Roxicotten, Roxies, 512s.

Pharmacology: The science that deal with understanding drugs and their actions.

Physical Dependence: The body's physiologic adaptation that becomes dependence to a substance.

Pink Cloud: An sense of euphoric feeling experienced those in early recovery from alcohol or drugs. The individual experiences overtly positive and optimistic thoughts and attitudes.

Placebo: A substance that has positive effects as a result of a patient's perception, that it is beneficial rather than as a result of a causative ingredient.

Post-Acute Withdrawal Syndrome (PAWS): The progression of addictive behavior that occurs, after the physical detoxification from drugs. This all begins with what I choose to give access. We tend to give permission to those things that are tempting to us. This is what I call

Pre-addiction Tendency: In our memory of past addictive behaviors and episodes, there remains an unintentional and often spontaneous recall. A remembrance of something good or pleasurable from our former life.

Precipitated Withdrawal Syndrome: Intensified or difficult withdrawal that is caused taking a substance that initiates withdrawal.

Prescription Drugs: A pharmaceutical drug that legally requires a medical prescription to be dispensed.

Psychedelic Drugs: Psychedelics are a hallucinogenic class of drug, whose primary action is to trigger psychedelic experiences such as visual and auditory changes and a altered state of consciousness. LSD, mushrooms and mescaline.

Psychoactive Drug: A psychoactive drug or psychotropic substance mainly used to describe drugs that alter ones mental process or behavior. Includes stimulants, depressants, hallucinogens. They create temporary changes in perception, mood, consciousness and behavior. Recreational or therapeutic uses. Highly addictive.

Psychological Dependence: This addiction represents the compulsion of the mind to drink or use based on a perceived need the substance fills. This facet of addiction can occur even if the person doesn't manifest other dependency indicators.

Psychotropic Drug: Any drug capable of affecting the mind, emotions, and behavior. Some legal drugs, such as lithium for bipolar disorder and illegal drugs such as cocaine.

Receptor: Protein on a target cell's membrane that a drug interacts with.

Recidivism: A repeated or frequent relapse into a previous condition or negative behavior. Refers especially to criminal behavior or drug use.

Recovery Rates: The percentage of addicted persons undergoing treatment who make progress in staying clean and sober.

Recovery: The process used in ending substance abuse. Refers also to a structure program designed to shape behaviors and actuate a lifestyle free from alcohol or drugs.

Relapse Prevention: An educational and sometimes therapeutic process used to assist recovering people from returning to their addiction.

Relapse: Returning to active addiction after a period of sobriety.

Reversed Tolerance: Reduced dosages of a prescribed drug produces a similar or the same effect that was achieved with a higher dose of the same drug.

Screening: A questionnaire of a persons life-history, with a focus on substance abuse and addictive behaviors. Normally followed by a professional interview to determine the extent of one's addiction, and possible treatment options.

Self-Help Group: Support Groups made up of recovering individuals dealing with similar issues that meet routinely to support each other and share their personal experience. Examples of this are AA, NA, Ala-non.

Side Effects: Secondary adverse effects of a prescribed drug; this can be found in non-prescription drugs as well.

Sobriety Accumulation Value: represents the length of time a person has been clean and sober and the value that they place on it.

Solvability Factor: We tolerate the same addiction challenges over and over, because we are not comfortable with the options available to bring a resolution.

Steroids: Performance-enhancing drug. A substance such as an anabolic steroid, human growth hormone that are used to improve athletic performance. Over use or misuse can have serious long term side effects.

Stimulant: Any drug that stimulates the brain or central nervous system, or excites bodily function. Stimulants induce alertness, elevated mood, spurts of energy, increased speech and motor activity. Will normally decrease appetite, used in weight loss.

Sublingual: Drugs that enter the blood through the membranes under the tongue.

Suboxone: A medication used to reduce symptoms of opiate addiction and withdrawal. This medication is similar to other opioid drugs, but it elicits relatively weaker effects than commonly-abused drugs like heroin and prescription painkillers like oxycodone. Street names Boxes, Sobos, Stops, Subs.

Substance Abuse (Chemical Dependence): Any use of drugs that is not in accordance with prescriptions or medical supervision. Normally descriptive of those who habitually abuse and develop an addiction or addict patterns.

Synthetic: Term that refers to non-organic, chemically synthesized, drugs that are not naturally occurring. Often found as unsafe recreational drugs.

Therapeutic Community: A structured mental treatment center, employing group therapy, individual counseling. Clients are encouraged to function within social norms and interact with people who have similar issues and support each other's recovery.

13th Stepping: A derogatory description of a more experienced member of a 12-step program, who makes romantic advances toward newcomer, under the pretense of helping them with sobriety.

Tolerance: Condition in which one must increase their use of a drug, in order for it to have the same effect.

Toxic Compassion: Allowing our compassion for the pain to override the need for a structured recovery process.

Toxicity: The plural of being toxic. Something poisonous. Refers to street drugs that have a high potential for overdose. Also misused prescription drugs have this capacity.

Tranquilizer: A drug that is used to reduce anxiety, fear, tension, agitation, and related states of mental disturbance and symptoms of severe psychosis.

Trigger: Common social, environmental or emotional situations that remind people in recovery of their past drug or alcohol use.

These experiences activate urges that may lead to a relapse into alcohol or drugs.

Uppers: See stimulants.

Urges: Similar to cravings but are less in urgency and can sometimes be suppressed by delayed gratification.

Unjustifiable Anger: This is being angry without a reason. Being angry all the time with a sense of entitlement and self-excusal.

Using: Describes the process of misuse of alcohol or drugs.

Vacillating Assistance Requiem: The term that describes a person who pretends to desire recovery, but doesn't do what is required to actually get sober. A performance to make them appear sincere.

Valium: A medicine of the benzodiazepine family that typically produces a calming effect. Used to treat anxiety disorders, alcohol withdrawal symptoms, or muscle spasms. Sometimes used with other medications to treat seizures. Street names, Foofoo, Tranks, Vallies.

Vicodin: Vicodin is a prescription medicine used for moderate to severe pain. Vicodin is a branded medication consisting of two major components, which are hydrocodone and acetaminophen. Street names, Vic, Vikes, Vees, Vitamin V. Has a high risk of overdose.

Withdrawal Symptoms: Severe, sometimes painful physical and emotional symptoms that generally occur after the person has discontinued drinking or using drugs for a period of time. Symptoms can include runny eyes, excessive yawning, a loss of appetite, panic attacks, sleeplessness, vomiting, shaking and irritability.

Withdrawal Syndrome: Combined physical reactions or extreme behaviors that result from the abrupt discontinuation of a drug or alcohol, that someone is addicted to.

Withdrawal: The sudden abeyance or interruption of a persons regular intake of alcohol, drugs, food or even a behavior.

Xanax: A drug that is used to treat anxiety and panic disorders. It promotes a feeling of calm and relaxation, and when taken correctly, is a safe and effective drug. Street names Z-bars, Planks.

BIBLIOGRAPHY QUOTES AND REFERENCES

Chapter 6, Page 85

"And you will know the Truth, and the Truth will set you free." John 8:32 (AMP)

Scripture quotations marked (AMP) are taken from the Amplified Bible, Copyright © 1954, 1958, 1962, 1964, 1965, 1987 by The Lockman Foundation. Used by permission.

"Then Jesus turned to the Jews who had claimed to believe in him. 'If you stick with this, living out what I tell you, you are my disciples for sure. Then you will experience for yourselves the truth, and the truth will free you.'" John 8:31-32 MSG

Chapter 10, Page 153

"Do not let anyone under pressure give in to evil by saying, "God is trying to trip me up." God is impervious to evil and puts evil in no one's way. The temptation to give in to evil comes from us and only us. We have no one to blame but the leering, seducing flare-up of our own lust." James 1:13-14 (MSG)

Scripture quotations marked MSG are taken from THE MESSAGE, copyright © 1993, 2002, 2018 by Eugene H. Peterson. Used by permission of NavPress. All rights reserved. Represented by Tyndale House Publishers, a Division of Tyndale House Ministries.

Chapter 7, Page 93

Singer/song writer, Paul Simon, wrote in one of his hits, “When I think back on all the crap I learned in high school, it’s a wonder I can think at all.”

© 1973 Words and Music by Paul Simon.

Bennighof, James (2007). The Words and Music of Paul Simon.

Greenwood Publishing Group. ISBN 978-0-275-99163-0.

Chapter 7, Page 98

“Eternal vigilance is the price of permanent sobriety.” George Campus

Chapter 8, page 2

(discursion) (noun) step by step philosophic reasoning, the act of discoursing or reasoning; as from thought to thought. It is the description of feeling, impact or solution”

Chapter 8, page 103

1200, cravan “defeated, vanquished, overcome, conquered,” apparently adapted from Old French cravent “defeated, beaten,”

DICTIONARY.COM UNABRIDGED

BASED ON THE RANDOM HOUSE UNABRIDGED DICTIONARY, © RANDOM HOUSE, INC. 2020

Chapter 8, Page 111

“Post-Acute Withdrawal Syndrome”. Much has been written about the subject of PAWS, and an expanded study is found in the book “What You Need to Know” by Terence T. Gorski

Copyright © 2020, Gorski Publications.

Chapter 10, Page 142

In 1994, there was a book called "A Clear and Present Danger". In the movie version of this story, the actor Harrison Ford, portrays a CIA Analyst named Jack Ryan. He is drawn into an illegal war fought by the U.S. government against a Colombian drug cartel.

Clear and Present Danger

ISBN: 9780399134401

Author/Editor: Clancy, Tom

Publisher: © Penguin US

NOTE:

The title was used a long time before the movie was made. It came into being in 1919. It was first announced by the U.S. Supreme Court as the "clear-and-present-danger doctrine". The concept of "clear and present danger" is a rationale for the limitation of free speech originated in a majority opinion written in 1919 by Supreme Court Justice Oliver Wendell Holmes.

It is a freedom of speech doctrine. I am not a legal expert by any means, but in general, it reflected an early standard by which the constitutionality of laws regulating subversive expression were evaluated in light of the First Amendment's guarantee of Freedom of Speech.

"The question in every case is whether the words used are used in such circumstances and are of such a nature as to create a clear and present danger, that they will bring about the substantive evils, that Congress has a right to prevent." (Speech could be punished if so.)

Made in the USA
Columbia, SC
30 September 2023